# THE CONATIVE CONNECTION

# THE CONATIVE CONNECTION

Uncovering the Link
between Who You Are
and How You Perform

## KATHY KOLBE

**Addison–Wesley Publishing Company, Inc.**
Reading, Massachusetts   Menlo Park, California   New York
Don Mills, Ontario   Wokingham, England   Amsterdam   Bonn   Sydney
Singapore   Tokyo   Madrid   San Juan

The terms Kolbe Conative Index™, Kolbe Concept™,
Niche for Knack™, Job-KCI™, Youth-KCI™, Thinkercise™,
and Action Mode™ are claimed as trademarks. Where
those terms appear in this book, they have been printed
in initial capital letters.

*Library of Congress Cataloging-in-Publication Data*

Kolbe, Kathy.
   The conative connection: uncovering the link between
who you are and how you perform / Kathy Kolbe.
      p.   cm.
   ISBN 0-201-51795-7
   1. Creative ability.   2. Will.   3. Self-actualization (Psychology)
4. Success—Psychological aspects.   I. Title.
BF411.K64   1990
153.8—dc20                                                        89-18003
                                                                      CIP

Cover design by Hannus Design Associates
Text design by Joyce C. Weston
Set in 11 point Palatino by Compset, Inc.,
Beverly, MA

**BCDEFGHIJ-DO-93210**
*Second printing, March 1990*

To the memory of my father, E. F. Wonderlic, who nurtured my creative instincts and taught me to value the freedom to be myself. Thanks, Dad, for egging me on.

# CONTENTS

# ACKNOWLEDGMENTS

You can search the early evening sky a long time and find only one or two stars. After a long wait, another appears, then the next, and then a few more. Those you squint at to keep in sight are finally joined by myriad stars that seem to appear all at once.

And so it's been with the Kolbe Concept. I'm grateful for the many who show their support now, but I am especially appreciative of those few stars who shone through during my lonely early efforts.

The first to share the responsibility and unrelenting sense of mission in helping people build on their natural talents was Paul Burgess, who became my partner. He has put into action the words "commitment" and "purpose." He has not only helped to clarify my abstract notions, he also proved the essential point that the Kolbe Concept was viable without Kathy.

Author, editor, and book reviewer Sheila Whalen was the first literary mind to grasp the significance of putting the Kolbe Concept into book form. Her practical and humor-filled perspective helped keep the project on course. Her constructive criticisms and other contributions helped immeasurably in bringing this book into being.

Sculptress Helen Blair Crosbie was the first person whose work validated my own. In her definitions of artistic talent I found another who recognized the universal nature of creativity. That she chose to publish her work with my company was an honor; that she is my good friend is a special joy.

While others knew I would be able to recover from a debilitating accident and write once again, Laurel McKiernan was the only one who knew just how difficult it would be to get to that point. She helped me return to fighting form, all the while accepting me in the shape I was in. Her special talent for nurturing those people others consider handicapped is a burden few of us could carry and a gift she shares unselfishly.

My husband, Will Rapp, an international expert, not only believed in the universal applications of the Kolbe Concept, he introduced it into numerous countries. He has been the ambassador who bridged cultural differences and the diplomat who has broadened my world view. He has also put into practice the very principles of humor, trust, and respect on which the concept is based.

These five stars gave me hope and great help. My children, Karen and David, gave me a hard time—which was often exactly what I needed in order to overcome the difficulties of trying to write once again. By not letting me off the hook for a commitment I made to complete this project, they told me they believed in me and that they valued what I had to say.

The synergy necessary to put this book into final form has come with the help of Kolbe Concept, Inc., team members, past and present. I owe a special debt to those whose talents were not well utilized; it's from my many management mistakes that I've gained the greatest understanding of the need to find better solutions.

I also appreciate the efforts of Jane Isay, George Gibson, and my agent, Gail Ross, who all trusted the scope of an unwritten concept, and my editor, Nancy Miller, whose cooperation and professionalism helped bring 1,400 pages down to those you'll read here.

Dozens of leaders in business, education, and government were willing to cooperate in the research necessary to validate the KCI. They were in the forefront, and therefore absorbed the brunt of nay-sayers' barrages. Their tenacity was proof of their dedication to the principles of individual accomplishment and group synergy—and their willingness to help bring conation into the light of day.

# PREFACE

Several years ago, a drunk driver going 55 miles an hour rammed into the back of a Volvo stopped at a traffic light. The two vehicles, totaled by the impact, spun across the intersection and into a third car, creating a tangle of metal and glass.

I was a passenger trapped in the back seat of that mangled but still protective Volvo. After being extricated from the compacted steel and rushed to the hospital, I was found to have broken bones and lacerations, but my mental abilities seemed to be intact.

The process of healing included many months of physical therapy. But, like so many personal crises, this ordeal also proved to be something of an opportunity and a source of profound insight.

In my first public appearance, months after the accident, I discovered its most devastating impact. I was moderating a business panel on educational issues, and was about to introduce the speakers from resumes they had just handed me. The letters on the page swam like amoebas under a microscope. My eyes and brain were conspiring against me like they had when I was a child, before I'd gained control over what was later diagnosed as dyslexia.

But the full impact of what had taken place didn't hit

me until almost a year after the accident, when I sat down to write a letter to my daughter, Karen.

"Dear Swijkn," I began.

I could no longer read or write with any consistency. The muscle relaxants I needed to take had somehow made me lose the eye coordination I had conquered through years of effort. Although in earlier years I had challenged my dyslexia by getting a degree from one of the toughest journalism schools in the country and earned my living as a writer, editor, and publisher, I found I now needed immense concentration just to sign my name. I knew I was going to have to "overcome" all over again.

Ironically, I had spent the preceding five years producing activity books for gifted children, books to help them use their minds productively. It was a bizarre twist that I now found myself using the materials I had designed for others to help me retrain my own mind.

It was eerie but fascinating to meet myself in this manner. It gave me the opportunity to test some of my own theories, to consider what about me had changed and what had remained the same.

Intellectually—or cognitively, if you will—I had been returned, at least in part, to a childlike state. Emotionally, I had suffered all the ups and downs you might expect of someone whose entire way of life had been disrupted. Yet there was a part of me that remained constant that neither the emotional strain nor the physical and intellectual impairment of the accident could alter.

Throughout the initial ordeal and the entire recovery process, I never once lost my capacity for striving after goals, nor my own distinctive ways of tackling the challenges that confronted me. When I could not even sit upright and had to be moved by a mechanical conveyer, my determination to rebuild my body's strength and dexterity led me to create challenges for myself. I painstakingly picked up pretzel pieces I had dropped on the floor by using a hand-operated arm-extender. I used spoons to flip balled napkins into paper cups I'd gotten others to place around the hospital room.

This is the way I had always been, even as a child—improvising, making deals. But what struck me most was the way the accident had isolated this "striving" part of me, the part that was not thinking or feeling, but simply doing. It had endured over time, and it had remained unchanged even through an upheaval that had altered so many other aspects of my being. Clearheaded or jumbled, happy or sad, optimistic or depressed, I had my own characteristic way of doing things, my own orientation toward action.

The book you are about to read defines the ways in which we all use our creativity and channel our mental energy to act and do. It is about a distinct part of the mind few of us have ever heard of, which was once the common currency of academic thought but was left behind in the face of seemingly more promising avenues of research about seventy-five years ago.

The part of the mind I've explored and now written about was accepted as a given by Aristotle and Plato, by Augustine and Spinoza. It is the part Immanuel Kant described as "practical reason"—the domain of action and the will, set apart from "pure reason" (the intellect) or "judgment" (the realm of feeling, pleasure, and pain). It is a cornerstone of almost every major system of Western thought having to do with human nature. From Plato to

Freud, action has always been seen as a separate domain of the mind, independent of but coequal to thinking and feeling.

But in the twentieth century, as behavioral and cognitive and developmental psychology diverged, and as other areas of the brain sciences became increasingly sophisticated, the study of the willing or active part of the brain was increasingly left behind.

Fortunately, that situation has now come full-circle, with work such as that by Gary Goldberg of Temple University School of Medicine, and Antonio R. Damasio of the University of Iowa College of Medicine. Their work and that of many others focuses on a region of the brain called the supplementary motor area (SMA), which they consider a significant factor in the development of the intention-to-act and the specification and elaboration of action. This region is part of the center brain, or "executive" brain, thought to provide a conduit between the medial limbic cortex and the primary motor cortex. According to Dr. Damasio, anatomical and functional knowledge of the SMA and its vicinity will someday "permit us to model the neuronal substrates of the *will*."

Scientific opinions vary greatly about the exact topography of the mind, and about the precise structures that might account for the behaviors I've studied and described. But my own work is much more pragmatic, dedicated to solving problems in the real world of human action, reaction, and interaction.

This book describes the method I've developed for identifying talent and targeting human effort, a method based on my observation of this hidden part of the mind in action. It is a new way of focusing creative energy, of dealing with change, and of predicting performance—of actually quantifying the probability of achievement in any particular endeavor. It helps create synergy out of conflict, and helps maximize mental energy by discovering and liberating our own most basic instincts for success.

Despite the fact that my theories and the index I've developed to measure ways of striving are now being incorporated into research in many institutions, my own initial research took place completely outside academia. I am not a neuroscientist or even a psychologist, rather a management strategist, an educational innovator, a specialist in creative learning, and an entrepreneur—but articulating the conative concept became more important than running a business. Most of all I am a crusader who believes each individual has his or her own destiny—a unique nature that persists through all life's struggles—and that, if we are free to act on our instinctive talents, every one of us will not only overcome obstacles but also achieve distinction and fulfill our sense of purpose.

My ideas will stand or fall on the power of their theoretical insight and on their practical value, not on the isolation of the particular anatomical structure or neurochemical pathway underpinning it. The proof is in the pudding. The action always speaks louder than words.

It's taken me four years since being pulled from that mangled car, but I was determined to write this book. I offer it to you as the best evidence I can provide that there is an internal power which allows all of us to do what we were meant to do.

**Conation** (koh NAY shun) n. Conation is the area of one's active mentality that has to do with desire, volition, and striving. The related **conatus** (koh NAY tus) is the resulting effort or striving itself, or the natural tendency or force in one's mental makeup that produces an effort. **Conative** (KOHN uh tiv) is the term in psychology that describes anything relating to conation. All these words come from the Latin *conatus*, past participle of the verb *conari* (to try). The Scottish philosopher William Hamilton (1788–1856) considered conation to be one of the three divisions of the mind, the one that included desire and volition, the other two being cognition (perception, awareness) and feeling. . . . Conation differs from velleity (the wish without the effort).

—*1000 Most Challenging Words*

# THE CONATIVE CONNECTION

# – 1 –

# Acting on Instinct

The player breaking down-court had all the right instincts for the up-tempo game. He was one of pro basketball's best guards, a guy who had proven he could rise to the occasion and make the clutch play, and here he was with the outlet pass and a chance to score, while the defense was scrambling to get set up. But just as he was about to break loose he saw the coach on his feet, waving his arms and shouting out signals, insistent on setting up the pattern. The player turned his head to listen, broke stride, and had the ball stripped from his hands.

Sitting in the Phoenix Coliseum that night, I cringed as I saw our team lose yet another chance to get into the game. Every night of the season had been like this. Talented players were being reined in, their instincts squelched, as the coach's perfectly valid instinct for structure was pushed too hard. After years of working in the area of enhancing human performance, watching these games was like witnessing some perverse case study in how to do everything wrong.

I went back to my office the next day and called the team's general manager. "I can't stand it anymore," I told him. "Please . . . let me help."

And that is how I began an association with one of my most visible clients, in the unlikely role of consultant on player selection for the NBA Phoenix Suns.

Within two basketball seasons, with a new coach who understands the power of instinctive action and management that encourages building on it, the Suns had moved from near the cellar of their league to status as a force to be reckoned with—one of the most improved teams in the history of the NBA. Which is just the kind of turnaround I'm used to seeing in the workplace whenever my clients discover and then go with the innate strengths of their managers and employees.

Abraham Maslow, the guru of self-actualization, said that man seeks "to be true to his own nature, to trust himself, to be authentic, spontaneous, honestly expressive, to look for the sources of his action in his own deep inner nature." He also said that "capabilities clamor to be used and cease their clamor only when they are used sufficiently."

This book offers you the groundbreaking opportunity to maximize your capabilities by recognizing the power of your own will—and *won't*. It will help you discover the instincts that drive capabilities, the sources of action, the authentic expressions of self that you need to trust in yourself and others. No longer will you find yourself taking debilitating detours as you search for your path of least resistance. You'll be spared the frustration of wondering why what works for your boss doesn't help you close the deal. You'll understand how and why your creative urges can generate productive effort, and how conflicts can be turned into synergy. You'll find validation for what you've known all along: that you have a unique way of doing things that works when you get to use it. And you'll be confronted with something you may not have realized—that others don't have to follow your example in order to do as well as you do.

The problem in Phoenix was a by-the-book coach stifling the instincts of more intuitive players, but that's just one variation on a much larger theme. You can see the same basic squandering of human potential when a crisis-driven entrepreneur waits until the last minute and then expects his controller to find new financing overnight. You see the same misguided expectations when a bunch of great "idea people" come up with blockbuster marketing concepts but no one's keeping inventory on the shelves. Or when the boss keeps hiring clones of himself. Or when a father tells his son to get his nose out of the encyclopedia and go play football with the other guys. Or when a wife thinks her husband who's smart enough to be a lawyer ought to be smart enough to fix the lawnmower. Or when a husband expects his wife to automatically be the one to keep up with everyone's birthdays and all the kids' dental appointments.

All it takes is having more than one child to know that all of us are born with unique ways of approaching everything we touch, and that even two people brought up in the same environment take on the world in vastly different ways. Unfortunately, this common-sense reality has been lost in the notion that we can be anything we want to be—if only we have the right schooling, the best therapists, and the financing behind us.

The Kolbe Concept is a practical approach to creative problem-solving that not only helps you discover the source of actions in your deep inner nature, but also shows you how to build on those strengths. Unlike psychological self-help books or popularized management theories, this is a concept which does *not* try to change you. Instead, this book explains why the key to success is in trusting your instincts.

There's more to achievement than what you know you ought to do, or what you wish you could do. There is also that which by your very nature you simply *will* and *won't* do. We all know you don't have to teach a cat to chase mice. You can, in fact, waste a lot of time trying to teach a cat *not* to chase mice, and even more trying to get it to bring you your slippers. When all is said and done, it is instinctive action that most truly speaks louder than words.

My own search for ways to build on innate talents led fifteen years ago to my founding a publishing company that offers kids options that challenge their creativity. I developed Thinkercise learning materials, books, and games that use children's problem-solving abilities to allow them to pursue knowledge through individual paths. Teachers find that children perform beyond grade level when able to map their own efforts through this variety of creative alternatives. Now I'm working with businesses throughout the world, using this same concept to analyze their options and improve bottom-line productivity.

Throughout this period, I've carefully observed human behavior, both in the classroom and in the business world.

It became clear to me that being intellectually gifted didn't determine what a person would *do*. Some smart kids wouldn't read directions, while others wouldn't do anything until they read them completely. Some experienced employees would count every marble in inventory and others would "guesstimate."

By focusing on how people actually succeeded, as opposed to how well they followed instructions, I found that there were different knacks, or capabilities, that propelled people toward their goals. I discovered that achievement multiplied when individuals of any age or status were able to use their knacks for getting things done. These knacks, I realized, were so basic that they were, in fact, instinctive—the human "wills and won'ts" that determine not what we think or feel or what we wish or hope, but how we most naturally deal with detail, with structure, with risk, and with the three-dimensional world. These creative instincts determine our most natural way of approaching problem solving, of arranging ideas or objects, and of using time and energy.

I observed that people's actions clustered into four sets of behaviors, or Action Modes, as I came to call them. The behaviors within each set did not overlap with the others and were distinguishable from them.

After years of observing and cataloging actions, interactions, and reactions, I became convinced that every intended response fit into one of the four modes. That I later found the ancient philosophers had recognized that human will was channeled through modalities was validation of the concept I had arrived at independently. That there was an almost universal agreement that four forces exist within the driving mechanism of the human being was also an after-the-fact revelation that I found reinforced my conclusions.

But, most of all, the validity of my work was confirmed when I found I could predict behavior with an accuracy that astounded even me. I could dissect the process any person went through when striving toward a goal and define each volitional act as coming from one of the four Action Modes:

**Fact Finder:** Precise, judicious and thorough, this mode deals with detail and complexity, seeking to be both objective and appropriate. Keen at observing and at gathering information, people who lead with this mode sometimes discover that information—facts—means more to them than to others. Sometimes they can be too judicious, seeming overly cautious as they wait for more data.

**Follow Thru:** Methodical and systematic, this mode is focused and structured, and brings order and efficiency. People who lead with this mode are meticulous at planning, programming, and designing, and predictability is essential to their being. Every organization needs people who lead with this strength in their operations, accounts receivable, and design functions. Obviously, there are times when an intense need for order can get out of hand.

**Quick Start:** With an affinity toward risk, this mode is spontaneous and intuitive, flexible, and fluent with ideas. People who lead with this mode are deadline- and crisis-oriented. They need an atmosphere of challenge and change, and sometimes they can be impatient.

**Implementor:** Hands-on, craft-oriented, this mode brings tangible quality to actions. People who lead with this mode have a strong sense of three-dimensional form and substance and the ability to deal with the concrete.

There was no effort that fell outside these clusters of actions or that couldn't be categorized within them. Their use did not correlate with levels of education, age, amount of training, or experience. Nor did genetics seem to offer an answer; siblings do not necessarily respond in the same manner to the same stimuli. The intellect didn't seem to be a factor, either; children of similar IQs studying in the same classroom reacted differently to educational demands. Nor did it seem to emanate from personality, as I observed there were both aggressive people and shy people who operated best through each mode, as well as happy and sad people.

## The Power of Will

The modern-day nonsense of categorizing people as "thinkers," "feelers," or "doers" ignores common sense and historical evidence that these faculties are not mutually exclusive. Everyone has an urge to make things happen—be those things good or bad, smart or dumb. We have an indomitable will that powers our instincts to act.

*The instinct to probe* makes us initiate Fact Finder activity.

*The instinct to pattern* forces us into Follow Thru behavior.

*The instinct to innovate* drives Quick Start energy.

*The instinct to demonstrate* comes out through Implementor actions.

Once I understood that the actions I'd observed and measured were instinctive, I also knew that they were the capabilities that Maslow and Spinoza and Kant and a multitude of philosophers had sought to identify. But I still didn't know that what I had discovered was the answer to a puzzle that had so mystified scholars—perhaps because they lacked practical business experience.

The importance of these instincts first came home to me in my early days of running a publishing company, as I was trying to understand the nature of the creativity I was trying to encourage. I found myself sometimes hiring the right person and then putting him or her in the wrong job, not fitting that person's knack into the right niche. I looked at resumes, talked to references, conducted in-depth interviews, and used personality and ability testing instruments to size up what a person had to offer. What was I missing?

I got it wrong because I was leaving out the one most reliable variable—"I will" is more important than IQ. "I will" is more a driving force than "I wish." This was a distinctly different aspect of the mind—the power of the creative instinct, or will—set apart from thinking and feeling.

The distinction between volitional action and the intelligence and emotion faculties have been observed throughout the ages. It had also been given a name, one I'd never heard before, but which confirmed the universal nature of my observations. The actions that determine how one strives toward a goal had for centuries been known as conation—from the Latin verb *conari*, meaning to strive.

Marketing experts in the mid-20th century singled out the conative act as the clincher in the decision-making hierarchy: Intelligence helps you determine a wise choice, emotions dictate what you'd like to buy, but until the conative kicks in, you don't make a deal—you don't put your money where your mouth is.

Conation is our knack for getting things done. It is separate from a person's intelligence or personality type. Some people think before they leap, employing their cognitive mind before engaging conative energy. Others want something so desperately, their affective emotions cause the conative to kick in ahead of any cognitive assessment.

The time-honored three-faculty concept of the mind is as follows:

## Three-Faculty Concept

| COGNITIVE | AFFECTIVE | CONATIVE |
| --- | --- | --- |
| to know | to feel | to act |
| skills | personality | talent |
| thinking | feeling | willing |
| truth | beauty | goodness |
| thought | emotion | volition |
| epistemology | esthetics | ethics |
| knowing | caring | doing |
| thought | mood | behavior |

## The Creative Force

Too often potential is discussed in terms of its limitations: intelligence, education, experience. Yet we have all seen instances where those with average IQ scores out-shine geniuses in common-sense problem solving.

The difference has been conation.

Creativity, often considered out of the realm of every-day concerns, is a part of every one of us who benefits from the freedom to be ourselves.

By definition, to create is to bring into being, to cause to exist, to produce. Since every individual has conation, the ability to take action, every individual also has the capacity to create. Because one does it with facts and figures rather than with paints does not make it any less a part of the creative process.

I have witnessed creativity in the accountant bringing order out of the chaos of a client's record-keeping; in the young person elaborating on the old family recipe; in maintenance people taking the risk of jury-rigging a repair; in a scheduler finding alternatives when the airport was fogged in.

We have always known a "doer" when we have seen one, a person who tackles even the most difficult task. But, while learning theorists have taken a microscopic look at the process of acquiring knowledge, and psychiatrists have increased awareness of our emotional makeup, those in ivory towers have skirted a practical approach to understanding conation, the key to how thought and emotion is translated into action.

Without conation there is no product, only potential. Conation is the achievement aspect of ability, the process through which we fulfill our goals.

I thought back to the times in my own life when I was

all thumbs, the times when the pieces fit magically together, the times when the writing flowed, and the times when I could slug away for hours and get nowhere. I had excelled when I had been free to act according to my own insistent knack. Whenever I had been true to my conative instincts, I got work done without becoming mentally fatigued. Whenever I had applied my talents naturally it had been like tapping into a torrent of energy just waiting to flow.

For me, that natural flow meant unleashing an instinct to take on challenges, to innovate, and to discover patterns as I went. It meant not being held to specifics or getting caught up in justifications. In the case of this book, it meant using my talents to take over where others had left off decades ago. Now my challenge was to get to the bottom line of the conative connection. To do that, I had to find a way to help people discover the force of their natural talents.

## The Four Action Modes

Through observation and testing over many years, I've come to realize that everyone has some of each of the conative instincts and acts through all four modes. It's just that the intensities are different within each of us. We lead from different strengths, and the mix of those modes is what gives each of us our own ways of doing—our modus operandi or "MO." That, I decided, was the measurable bottom line.

## Conative Characteristics

**Fact Finder:** It is through the Fact Finder Mode that you are a pragmatist, prober, arbitrator, practitioner, researcher, judge, or realist.

Targeting your efforts through your strength in the Fact Finder Mode requires the freedom to:

| | | | |
|---|---|---|---|
| evaluate | prove | formalize | investigate |
| probe | inquire | deliberate | differentiate |
| calculate | justify | specify | prioritize |
| define | research | allocate | |

You will prevent stress and accommodate needs by using your Fact Finder Mode to act:

| | | |
|---|---|---|
| correctly | strategically | practically |
| thoroughly | expertly | deliberately |
| prudently | studiously | conclusively |
| tactfully | discerningly | appropriately |

**Follow Thru:** It is through the Follow Thru Mode that you are a planner, designer, regulator, pattern-maker, systematizer, theorist, programmer.

Targeting your efforts through your strength in the Follow Thru Mode requires the freedom to:

| | | | |
|---|---|---|---|
| arrange | design | chart | consolidate |
| translate | schedule | plan | provide service |
| budget | prepare | format | coordinate |
| structure | guarantee | integrate | |

You will prevent stress and accommodate needs by using your Follow Thru Mode to act:

| | | |
|---|---|---|
| consistently | dependably | methodically |
| systematically | routinely | comprehensively |
| fashionably | concisely | theoretically |
| efficiently | cautiously | continuously |

**Quick Start:** It is through the Quick Start Mode that you are a catalyst, generalist, innovator, entrepreneur, promoter, improvisor.

Targeting your efforts through your strength in the Quick Start Mode requires the freedom to:

| | | | |
|---|---|---|---|
| deviate | brainstorm | contrive | ad lib |
| intuit | originate | risk | play hunches |
| promote | change | devise | experiment |
| invent | challenge | abbreviate | |

You will prevent stress and accommodate needs by using your Quick Start Mode to act:

| | | |
|---|---|---|
| fluently | intuitively | imaginatively |
| decisively | insightfully | defiantly |
| rapidly | spontaneously | conceptually |
| flexibly | adventurously | inventively |

**Implementor:** It is through the Implementor Mode that you are a molder, builder, handcrafter, athlete, manufacturer, agriculturalist, artisan.

Targeting your efforts through your strength in the Implementor Mode requires the freedom to:

| craft | repair | render | use physical effort |
| construct | display | shape | demonstrate |
| master | mold | form | put together |
| build | practice | | |

You will prevent stress and accommodate needs by using your Implementor Mode to act:

| skillfully | mechanically | athletically |
| tangibly | strenuously | physically |
| sturdily | handily | demonstrably |
| technically | dexterously | substantively |

No matter how useful it may be to use this shorthand account, the four Action Modes do not represent "types" of people, rather aspects of us all. Any mind can operate in every mode, using each of the skills attributed to that mode. The variables are intensity, reliability, and effectiveness without stress.

Even with this rudimentary insight into the conative domain, I could see why a person who is hard-working and driven to achieve, who organizes massive projects and brings home lots of bacon, might not ever lift a hand to fix a broken faucet. Why some executives carefully outline a subject while others scribble triggered thoughts. Why those who tinker with tools often choose to make no comment on their constructions. Why planning sessions seem silly to some and totally necessary to those who already have plans. Why some executives insist on feasibility studies and others flee from them in terror. Why "focus" is the key to some people's tennis game and the way to self-conscious frustration for others.

Discovering the Creative Instincts and the Action Modes was a breakthrough that helped me understand why two secretaries who both typed 80 words a minute, both took shorthand at 120, and both had made good grades in school, could contribute so unequally on the job. But I still needed a way to keep from hiring the wrong one.

Working closely with the leadership of multi-national companies, unions, professional firms, and educational and nonprofit groups, I have found that problems and opportunities inevitably center on conative issues. More than 80 percent of lost productivity was clearly caused by the use or misuse of strengths in the Action Modes—the universal characteristics that are the same for the file clerk, the surgeon, and the longshoreman, the same in any culture on any continent. They were nothing less than a new common denominator in our understanding of human nature.

Equally important, they were bedrock, something that did not change over time the way our conflicting ideas and emotions do. Yet here we were spinning our wheels every day, trying to bend these instincts into conformity, erase them, overcome them, or cover them up, when what we needed was to see them as an incredibly powerful source of energy to be harnessed.

It was when I began delving back into psychology and philosophy to explore this concept of action instincts that I came across the curious fact I alluded to before, that the conative connection had been known, yet not fully explained. Through the centuries, thinkers ranging from Plato to Spinoza, Hobbes, Descartes, Kant, Hume, Freud, and Piaget all accepted the three-part structure of the human mind. They recognized the conative as just as important as intelligence or personality in making sense of the individual.

The conative for these philosophers was the source of all striving, longing, ambition, and self-expression. It was the root of a person's persistence against obstacles, the very essence of the person, for it is through conation that we strive toward goals or self-actualize. And it is through the conative that one is productive, for as Hume and others point out, intellectual awareness alone cannot move us to do anything.

It was the discovery of this long history that made me fully realize the significance of the conative connection. Which astounded me, even angered me. For whatever reason, once Binet had quantified intelligence in the early part of this century, researchers—even Piaget, who found the conative the mental domain most difficult to differentiate—lost interest in the more elusive concept of striving. What had been the accepted wisdom fell out of favor. University scholars told me: "We don't study conation anymore. It's considered archaic." Psychologists cautioned me that discussing the will had become outdated and was only making a slight comeback in non-traditional circles. Stanford's Richard Snow differed: "The conative seems to have dropped out of modern psychology's consciousness. It deserves reinstatement and research."

The problem that had discouraged Piaget was differentiating the conative from the affective personality and the cognitive intelligence. This barrier, as well as an inability to define conative modes, had apparently kept academics thinking about thinking and psychologists worrying about feelings. It was left to an entrepreneur like me to do something about doing.

As the daughter of E. F. Wonderlic, the originator of the concept of personnel testing, I had been involved with psychometric measurement most of my life. Unlike most people who might follow their curiosity, I was able to design the necessary pencil-and-paper test, a way to index this striving part of the mind that was altogether different from the mental ability my father had quantified. Dad had always agreed there was more to what made a person tick than mere intelligence and personality. Now I could prove it.

What I developed is called The Kolbe Conative Index (KCI), a disarmingly simple way of measuring the distribution and intensity of the four Action Modes within each individual. It takes most people only a few minutes to complete and provides easy-to-use results. It doesn't tell how a person thinks or feels or how much they know or what they value—those are attributes on the cognitive and affective levels which the KCI strips away.

What the KCI does tell you is what a person, left to his own devices, will *do.*

I've now tested 20,000 individuals on five continents and from all walks of life and I've used the KCI to restructure businesses across the United States, Canada, Australia, and Europe. On every continent, I've found evidence of the universal nature of conation. People everywhere acted on the same four instincts through the same Action Modes. Cultural variations influence career decisions, and economic and political conditions have an impact on opportunities, but the internal drives and natural talents are distributed equally everywhere.

Oddly enough, even with just the four primary modes, and even when the subject is themselves, people's guesses as to their own MOs are wrong about 50 percent of the time. But, of the thousands of subjects to whom I've given the KCI assessment and fully explained the system, only a handful have ever responded that the results did not accurately reflect how they function.

In fact, whenever I consult now with organizations or individuals, my ideas trigger recognition in almost everyone, the "Aha!" that comes when you present a truth that simply feels right to people, that matches up with their gut reaction. The real breakthrough in credibility, however, comes with the realization that what I've developed is an assessment of human behavior patterns which is not only accurate, but both quantitative and predictive.

Over the years, the test and its results have been validated and proven to be reliable. Proving its ability to predict performance, the KCI has singled out those individuals who would be prone to industrial accidents, those who will comply with regulations, those who won't. It clarifies why a person with strength in Quick Start rebels against Fact Finder educational programs, why management by objectives makes sense for some and "walking-around" management is the answer for others. The conative connection finally puts to rest the issue of why time management never will "take" for everyone—yet explains why there will always be those who insist it is absolutely necessary.

The predictive validity of the KCI was obvious every time I showed a result to a group of co-workers and they could single out who it depicted, or when I could use it to forecast how a particular person would respond to a situation and he or she would do just as I had predicted, or when I would interpret otherwise unapparent stresses and have them confirmed.

That such information related to innate strengths was corroborated with in-depth interviews, twin studies, and repeated examinations. When people retook the KCI, no matter how many months or years later, the results were within the 5 percent margin of error on the KCI.

Perhaps the most telling research was finding a natural distribution, or bell curve, for each mode in a general population—and seeing the variation from it by career path. Men and women, youths and senior citizens, retarded and gifted, white and black all have equal conative power or mental energy. How they used it varied dramatically. Those who have the freedom to follow their instincts find self-fulfillment. Those who don't suffer lack of self-esteem and a loss of sense of self.

I include the KCI on page 199, and I recommend that you take the test for the specificity it affords and the validation it provides of the nature of your own strengths. Nonetheless, you don't need the KCI to benefit from this book. You can go a long way on common sense and careful observation, absorbing the applications for this kind of insight into your daily vocabulary and even your worldview.

Understanding the instinctive nature of conation is a valuable first step toward learning to unleash and target mental energy, and toward discovering and directing the different forms of creativity within yourself or within any group of people. You'll find that a basic grasp of the conative connection will enable you to work more intensely without stress, by shifting gears among different types of creativity when you're stuck for the long haul and might otherwise burn out. You'll find that it improves communication, because conation helps you understand what drives both the speaker and the listener and how they'll respond to differing directives or appeals.

Unfortunately, we're still swimming against the tide of the same old world that never took these distinctive ways of doing into account. From the earliest parental influence to the moment we enter the school system to the moment we retire, the world conspires to enforce only one way. "The way *I* was brought up." "The curriculum as it's written." "According to standard operating procedures." So much mental energy has gone into simply persisting and overcoming all the obstacles presented by a world determined to work against us. None of us, given a clear range of options, would choose to live our lives fighting just to be who we are, instead of using our talents for more productive purposes.

Why do we have so many clichés about square pegs in round holes and barking up the wrong tree? Parkinson's Law and the Peter Principle? Because most people are forced to go through life as a blunder hunt. This book is an attempt to change all that, and to share with a much wider audience the same insights and techniques I offer my corporate clients.

How do you know what you'll be good at? You can proceed by trial and error and waste a lifetime trying to find the answer. What should you look for in a relationship? Who should you hire for that job? What kind of team do you need in research and development? How can you work out a deal with your teenager?

In this book I don't narrowly isolate the business or career implications of the conative connection, but rather try to focus on the whole person. After all, it's when we've used up certain energies at the office that we have none of that mode left to give at home.

The measurable results of using the Kolbe Concept include athletes dramatically improving their records, salespeople bringing in more than 200 percent in new business, managers cutting turnover in half and cutting stress-related absenteeism altogether, students being able to get better grades, and companies reaching productivity goals for the first time in years.

There are, however, benefits which cannot easily be quantified. The cost of not knowing your creative power, of having your personal performance inhibited and your contribution denied, cannot be measured in numbers.

Gratifying as it is to spend the day with a CEO, helping him to isolate the conative strengths of the people on his organizational chart and build productive teams with the right leadership, what means much more to me is the number of these tough-guy bosses who will close their doors and share how the Kolbe Conative Concept has made a difference in their own lives, how trusting their instincts has opened their eyes to a new definition of success: the freedom to be yourself.

# – 2 –

# Taking Initiative

Imagine lying in bed in the early hours of a spring morning, half-asleep and half-awake, because the room's turned cold and now you're uncomfortable. You know there's a nice warm blanket at the foot of the bed, but you can't quite bring yourself to reach down and pull it up.

No matter how much you wish you could get warm or how well you know the simple steps necessary to reach that objective, you won't solve your problem until you take initiative and actually reach down and pull up that blanket. That's when you engage your conative self—when you get beyond thinking and feeling and commit your mental energy to action.

Everyone has an equal capacity of conative striving mechanisms or mental energy, to direct toward action. My studies with people from all over the world indicate that the Action Modes do not discriminate by sex, age, race, or educational level. We all have Fact Finder, Follow Thru,

Quick Start and Implementor abilities, and we all have the potential to use our own distinctive combination of those modes for equally productive lives. The problem is that not all of us are using it to our advantage.

## Creative Modes

Early in my work on conation I believed Quick Start was the mode through which people initiate action. I spent many months testing this belief before realizing I was wrong. My own conative bias had misled me. Having a lot of Quick Start, I usually initiate action intuitively, by originating methods and taking on challenges.

But all of our acts are the expression of our individual creative instincts—our conative self. Our goal-directed efforts are attempts to bring our thoughts and feelings into being. We don't accomplish this just by innovating; we do it when we probe, pattern, or demonstrate.

As I worked with people throughout the world in a variety of circumstances, it became clear that the creative process begins with a person's most dominant mode, whichever that may be. Often, creative problem-solving begins by probing what isn't working, or by setting priorities. Fact Finders initiate activity in this way—by setting agendas, outlining proposals, and clarifying needs. A Follow Thru might establish a theory or plan as the first step in achieving goals, putting matters in context before going off in new directions, or integrating disparate elements into a whole. The Quick Start creates by trying something new, or coming up with alternatives. Implementors initiate by shaping a form or model, or through a physical demonstration.

Within the individual there is a kind of internal synergy that can come from learning how to make the best of the four talents. By learning to recognize when and how to engage each aspect of your own mental energy, you can push your creativity beyond the limits you thought possible.

You can use the conative connection to isolate the four distinct parts of your own creativity and bring them all into the game, but you start the internal creative process with whatever mode is your strong suit.

## Degrees of Effort

Why do some people have to put a lot of effort into straightening up a room, while others keep it tidy as they go? What's behind one person easily managing a diversity of projects and another who's just as bright finding it tough to do more than one thing at once? The answer is that there are degrees of each Action Mode in each individual that determine the amount of energy available for different types of activity.

You have some Quick Start capacity, but do you have enough to keep a dozen projects going at once? Some people simply have to keep a lot of balls in the air while others dig in their heels when you try to get them to take on too much all at once. You have Implementor ability but when is the last time you volunteered to operate heavy equipment? Any equipment?

I have found it possible to distinguish three levels of performance for each Action Mode. People either insist on doing things in a certain way, resist those same activities, or are willing to accommodate themselves to them.

*Resistant* does not mean an inability to act within a mode—anyone can follow procedures. It means you won't act that way of your own volition.

A resistant Fact Finder will try to use his new computer with as little help from the manual as possible. He won't figure out all its options before starting in, and probably won't discover for two years that it has all sorts of "bells and whistles" he didn't know were there.

A resistant Follow Thru won't buy groceries until she's run out of a necessity. She may clip coupons, but is unlikely to have them with her when she finds herself at the store.

Resistant Quick Starts won't plunge into water or a new business or a game. "What's your hurry?" they'll ask if pushed, sensing they're best to avoid anything that comes at them too fast.

A resistant Implementor won't dig up the soil for a garden or have a home workshop, or tinker with the car if he can avoid it. He probably won't have the right tools even if he needs to fix something.

Resistance means that, while you may be able to get by in a certain mode, you'll be dragging your feet or overcompensating all the way, and if you have to operate there for too long a period, the stress of going against your grain will sooner or later lead to burnout. Your resistant mode will never be where you'll shine. You need to find ways around having to use it.

*Insistent* means that given free rein, this is how you *will* proceed, as naturally and intensely as a cat chasing a mouse. This is where you need to be most of the time. This is where you will soar.

*Accommodating* means going with the flow. You can

function comfortably in this mode, using it as needed, and, while you probably won't be a leader or a star here, you won't feel stress, either.

An insistent Follow Thru creates systems; an accommodating Follow Thru will stay with the system. A resistant Follow Thru may stay with the system for a period of time, feeling great stress, but will eventually burn out and exit the system. An insistent Quick Start initiates change; an accommodating Quick Start can cope with change; but a resistant Quick Start drags his heels trying to avoid it.

When I designed the KCI, I set the total capacity of mental energy for any given individual at 20 units of conative power. One unit thus equals 5 percent of total mental energy. Everyone acts in all four modes from time to time, and no one makes a majority of his or her mental effort in any one mode; in fact, I found that 50 percent, or 10 units of a possible 20, was the highest degree of effort anyone could make in a single mode. I therefore assigned a scale of 1 to 10 to measure the intensity of each of the four Action Modes within each individual. A 10 in any mode is the greatest insistence, the mid-range (4–6) is the accommodating zone, and a score of 3 or less indicates a person's resistance to doing things that way. Being highly accommodating, at the 6 level, means a person is more likely to take on a task requiring such actions than simply do it if necessary. The KCI of any person thus generates a four-digit score—the individual's modus operandi.

The KCI score on page 27 is for a person who leads with Quick Start energy but has a strong second suit in Fact Finder. This person is resistant to Follow Thru, and mildly accommodating in Implementor. His modus operandi would be expressed as 6384. This means 6 in Fact Finder,

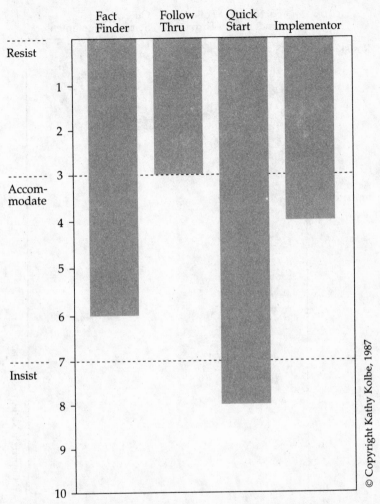

The KCI doesn't pigeonhole you. No one is *all* of any one mode. Fifty percent of mental energy—10 units out of a possible 20—was the highest degree of effort I found anyone could make in a single mode.

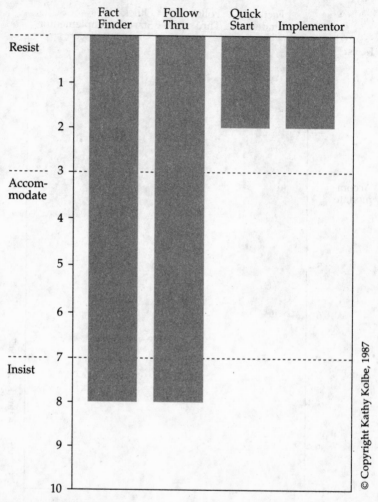

It is possible to have two insistent modes, which would result in off-setting resistances in other modes.

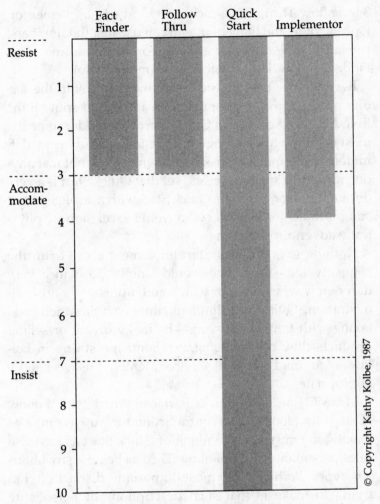

People who are called strong-willed often have a mode of strong insistence.

3 in Follow Thru, 8 in Quick Start, and 4 in Implementor. Once you get the hang of it, you can use just the numbers, provided you always keep the order the same—Fact Finder, Follow Thru, Quick Start, Implementor.

Even when a person leads with one strong suit, the second most intense mode puts quite a different spin on the first. My research shows Quick Start/Fact Finder to be the most common MO among entrepreneurs, who by my definition are people who risk their own capital, not just anyone running a small business, yet that Quick Start is a very different person from the Quick Start with a strong second suit in Implementor—one who would excel in more physically adventurous settings.

Nothing says a Quick Start/Implementor can't run the company too—he or she would simply do it in a very different way, with less research and more hands-on demonstration. Quick Start/Implementors combine their risk-taking with tangible pursuits—be it sky diving or selling products they can demonstrate. Someone strong in Follow Thru might find a service-oriented business more appropriate.

My MO is 2684, Quick Start combined with Follow Thru. If that looks like a contradiction to you, you may be making the mistake of thinking of Quick Start as having a sales personality and of Follow Thru as being a shy librarian type. Perhaps the most important distinction I'm trying to make is that such descriptions of personality have nothing to do with talent or knack or striving—with conation. Conation is an entirely separate domain of the mind. It is neither thinking nor feeling, neither left brain nor right, rather the center brain, which is triggered into action by these others. Personality can camouflage the underlying conative truth, and sometimes lead to symptoms of what are, in reality, conative problems.

Resistances sometimes lead to guilt. An executive who resists both Fact Finder and Follow Thru had a recurring nightmare in which he saw himself lost on a university campus unable to locate the proper classroom until he'd missed a lecture and found gibberish printed on an assignment sheet. After twenty years of waking up in a cold sweat, he discovered that knowing his MO gave him permission to not worry about going back to get an M.B.A. The nightmare stopped.

Some months ago, executives at a public utility company asked me to talk with a young electrical engineer who was an important part of their strategic planning. They thought of him as one of their star performers, and they were all set to invest big dollars in sending him off to a leading-edge training program. Their plan was to send him out of state for a year of extensive knowledge-transfer from a major supplier. But lately he'd developed an attitude problem that troubled his managers. That's where I stepped in.

"It's not fair," he told me, anxious to justify his position. Since his relocation allowance and total compensation was very, very generous, I asked him to clarify what was bothering him.

As we spoke, the real issue surfaced. He was single and therefore he wasn't going to get the same incidental cost-of-living compensation as the engineers who were married.

"That's inappropriate," he kept saying. And what he

found most inappropriate was that the terms varied, however slightly, from the details of the agreement on which he'd based his decision to go. Despite the fact that the company was making every effort to accommodate him and being very generous in the process, he considered any change whatsoever to be entirely unacceptable.

The manager who had asked me to step in could not cope effectively with this situation because he did not understand the young engineer's conative make-up, or the concept underlying it, for that matter. A Quick Start himself, he thought the challenge alone should be enough to motivate the young man. What he didn't understand was that being young—or a man—does not necessarily equate with being adventurous.

As it turned out, the young engineer was highly insistent in Fact Finder and just as highly resistant in Quick Start. Dotting *i*'s and crossing *t*'s means a great deal to Fact Finders; pushing the limit does not. In fact, to a resistant Quick Start, change per se can be a source of functional stress.

If the manager had known the young man's MO, if even the young man himself had been more in tune with his own conative needs, the communications problems and ill feelings could have been avoided.

The KCI gives us insight into our most productive ways to perform, as well as cautioning us on actions we need to avoid.

## Clues to Conative Nature

It's simply not possible, of course, to have a KCI score on everyone you know, but by careful observation of the ways someone initiates activity, what he or she will or won't do when given the freedom to be himself, it is often possible to detect the most insistent and resistant modes in his or her MO. I haven't given the KCI to any of our past presidents, for example, but I can make some educated guesses.

Ronald Reagan was a promoter, not an administrator. This is strong Quick Start leadership with a resistance to Fact Finder. His stellar performances were in the crunch, when he got people to "do it for the Gipper." He created a problem, though, by surrounding himself with too many other Quick Starts with the same resistance. Everybody in his inner circle was satisfied with information that could be summarized on a file card.

John Kennedy was perhaps Reagan's conative opposite. He was the sort who wanted to plan for every contingency. He was slow to take decisive action in the Cuban missle crisis because he couldn't get enough information. Nothing was left to chance with JFK, who proved by withdrawing air support at the Bay of Pigs that risk was not his strong suit. He was a Fact Finder who drew from history and asked his speech writers to include both literary quotes and lots of data in every script.

Jimmy Carter, the former nuclear submarine engineer, was given a carpentry set by his staff when he left the White House. He retired to farmland, to making furniture, and to refurbishing houses for the poor. I would describe him as a Fact Finder/Implementor who hadn't enough Quick Start to lead through a period of change. He often worked eighteen-hour days, reserving every detail for himself, but lacked both an ability to sell his ideas and to function efficiently.

Anybody who watched *Saturday Night Live* during the Ford years saw the President depicted as tripping off planes and zapping golf balls in unpredictable directions. But Jerry Ford was also a renowned college football player. I think Ford was a Facilitator (see p. 37), accommodating in each mode, whose clutziness was a bum rap. A more insistent person might not have been able to get the consensus to pull the country through one of its worst political nightmares.

Psychologists have said that Nixon hid behind a mask. My own assessment is that he was a Fact Finder resistant in Quick Start who was incapable of dealing with the bottom line. Opening relations with China has been called a bold stroke, but it was certainly no gut-level action. Everything was the result of cold calculation with Nixon as he worked in his side office, filling legal pads with analyses and instructions. While Nixon and Kennedy may have shared insistences and resistances, they may have had different second suits, Nixon's being Follow Thru and Kennedy's his Implementor recreational outlets.

Lyndon Johnson's Fact Finder seemed limited to knowing how many votes were out there, as he bypassed protocol and also dodged Follow Thru procedures. Flooring his Cadillac over dusty back roads or lifting his shirt to show a surgical scar or hauling his dogs up by their ears, he always dealt with things in his own Quick Start/Implementor way.

While guessing your own or anyone else's MO is difficult at best, there are clues to conative nature that you can learn to observe, and ways of coping you can learn to use in managing your own time and energy and recognizing how others need to function. The Kolbe Conative Concept identifies the cause and effect of actions so your expectations of yourself and others can match realities. It gives you permission to be your unabashed self.

If you use your mental energy to gather data, you're probably *insistent in Fact Finder*. If you are so strong-willed about having detailed information and acting on experience, you might be driving other people nuts. They may complain that you slow down decision-making by your insistence on greater specificity. They might even accuse you of indecisiveness, but it's just that you can't justify doing something without being sure it's the right thing. No matter how much others may complain about pedantry, you've averted many a disaster because you read the fine print.

But what about the person who won't justify himself and finds having to be precise a waste of effort? This is the most obvious sign of someone *resistant in Fact Finder*, just as likely to drive others up the wall—merely a different group. Given freedom to be yourself, you simply won't argue about the data. You'd rather not get reimbursed if it means spending time filling out the accident report. Often you don't know how you know something, or why you did something, and you really don't care too much about what's appropriate. You may not delegate or manage well because you may unwittingly withhold vital pieces of the puzzle. You're at your best rounding off, guesstimating, and getting on with it.

If you need to make a list and check it twice, you're probably *insistent in Follow Thru*. Like Felix in *The Odd Couple*, you expect the spices to be in alphabetical order. You might be considered finicky, but you are a master of focused attention. You're at your best doing one thing at a time and completing it before moving on to another, and accordingly you find distractions incredibly frustrating. You not only embrace structure, you need it. You see the rhythms and patterns around you, and you're in your own game when you can align the rhythms inside you with the rhythms of external demands.

On the other hand, trouble focusing mental energy probably means *resistance in Follow Thru*. Some may say you're distractible; others that you know how to "let go" and get on with your life. You have a compelling need to avoid structure, being boxed in, or having to concentrate on one thing for very long. Some may consider you inefficient, but your ability to cope with open-endedness is essential to your effectiveness.

Maybe you thrive on challenges but get bored easily. If so, that's the *insistent Quick Start* in you showing through. You take risks and have many projects happening all at once, often creating the chaos that others complain about having to clean up. You're at your best under deadline pressure, or when someone's just described the job as "Mission Impossible."

You don't work well on deadline? Playing a hunch isn't your game and you'd rather stick with the tried and true? Those signals point to *resistance in Quick Start*. You need to avoid crisis atmosphere or having to improvise.

If the best way for you to explain something is to show how it's done, you're probably *Implementor insistent*. Neither the spoken nor the written word is your medium, and you rarely sit still long enough for discussions. Your physical intensity may be expressed through sports, or carpentry, or overseeing manufacturing, or producing anything that's tangible. Quality control is your forte. But not all Implementor insistent people are found in steel mills or domed stadiums. You can be an Implementor insistent book publisher, although what compels you will more likely be the physical quality of the binding and the paper rather than the weekly editorial meeting.

If someone shrieks "Who in the world did this!" every time you try to fix something, that's *Implementor resistance*. You're not the natural athlete, you don't work well with wood, and you'd be better off hiring someone else to repair your car.

## The Facilitator

What if you are neither insistent nor resistant in any mode, but accommodating in all modes? This is the profile of the *Facilitator*. Facilitator is actually not a distinct mode, rather a very valuable ability to accommodate all of the others. This is the MO of the person who is adaptable, the supporting player who, as we all know, can win an Academy Award without having to star.

Facilitators' efforts are often taken for granted because they don't dominate in any situation where others have insistences. They're even-keeled conatively and don't rock boats. In fact, they're often criticized for a seeming lack of assertiveness. (There can be an affective overlay to the conative connection, causing the very problem of disengaging the two that kept Piaget and others from isolating the conative.) They stand out for their cooperative abilities. Others tend to rely on them to mediate because of

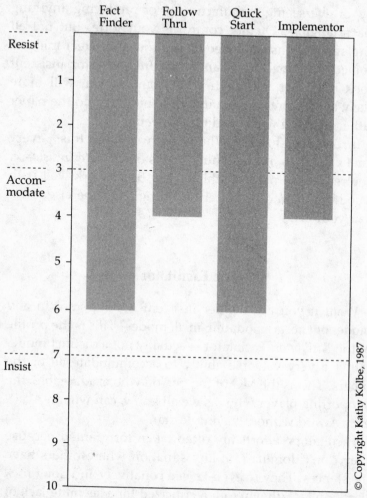

A Facilitator will have all four modes in the mid-range. The Facilitator can do things any way they need to be done, mixing and matching modes as necessary.

their innate talent for understanding all sides without having to take one. Because they are even-handed conatively, they can work with varying MOs without conflict. They can also be the glue that keeps others working together. By accommodating the needs of those individuals who are insistent or resistant in each of the modes, they keep energies targeted.

A law firm for which I was doing a seminar had many partners with highly insistent/resistant MOs. There were a lot of leaders who wanted to delegate, and no one who was willing to accommodate. With all those take-charge types, how did the firm manage without partner problems?

The secret weapon they had protecting them against conflicts was a Facilitator. This man was a wonder. He could sit back and recognize what was going on in each partner's head. He knew how to placate them, how to handle their particular needs. When the firm moved its offices, he facilitated it so those Fact Finders for whom files were most important had them at their fingertips throughout the process. He designed a system that appeased the Follow Thrus and came up with similarly appropriate solutions for the I-need-it-yesterday problems that would otherwise have been encountered with the Quick Starts.

Facilitators do things because they need to be done, which makes them particularly effective in team situations. They sense the needs of others and meet them by intercepting phone calls that might be troubling, doing the errand others might forget, having the tools there before they're even asked for, settling disputes by seeing all sides.

Their needs? People tend to think Facilitators can do it all without needing anything in return. They don't seem to tire as easily because they don't use up any single mode as fast as someone else might. But they do have needs. Their energy isn't boundless. They need to be let off the hook for the speeches or anything else that demands they be out front. And they need to be recognized for their contributions, even though their actions don't necessarily draw attention to them.

In any endeavor that draws highly insistent people there will be a need for Facilitators. That only 15 percent of the population has this MO makes it as scarce a commodity as insistence in any mode. We all have the potential of learning from our mistakes, but no insistent type is ever going to mellow conatively and be able to match the Facilitator at his own game.


## Natural Advantages

These descriptions, though useful, are stereotypes, because nobody is *all* of any one thing. There truly is no such thing as "can't"—but there are combinations of talent that make people better suited to one career than another. Each of us has some mental energy devoted to every one of the four Action Modes, combining in such a way as to give us seventeen different distinctive ways of operating— each of which can be depicted as a "knack."

Some people have a head for engineering. For others, it's "not their thing." With the thousands of KCI results I've observed, I've been able to statistically identify the conative traits that cluster in various career paths. The KCI has been refined to the point that it can even predict whether a person will most likely succeed as a trial attorney or a corporate lawyer. The particular combination of strengths in your MO is your personal leverage for getting things done. For example, dual strengths in Fact Finder and Implementor give a person a mechancial knack. The Fact Finder/Quick Start combination is the knack of the manager.

The following aren't meant to be job titles, rather frames of mind or methods of operation. For instance, a person may have a manager's mentality because of her MO, but be in an academic environment. She'll try to manage that situation. A technician in a manager's job will emphasize product quality over program development. An entrepreneurial person in the corporate world will try to break down the resistance to innovation. A Quick Start/Implementor mindset housed in a body without muscular strength will take physical risks with equipment that enhances that need—perhaps a motorcycle or an airplane.

## The Niche for Knack

| KNACK | NICHE |
| --- | --- |
| Fact Finder | researcher |
| Fact Finder/Follow Thru | strategic planner |
| Fact Finder/Quick Start | manager |
| Fact Finder/Implementor | technician |
| Follow Thru | designer |
| Follow Thru/Fact Finder | systems analyst |
| Follow Thru/Quick Start | program developer |
| Follow Thru/Implementor | manufacturer |
| Quick Start | sales promoter |
| Quick Start/Follow Thru | theorist |

| | |
|---|---|
| Quick Start/Fact Finder | entrepreneur |
| Quick Start/Implementor | pioneer |
| Implementor | artisan |
| Implementor/Fact Finder | mechanic |
| Implementor/Follow Thru | quality controller |
| Implementor/Quick Start | adventurer |
| Facilitator | mediator |

Your knack reflects how you will function on any job. No matter what your MO, for instance, you can take on a management role—it's not only the Fact Finder/Quick Starts who find themselves at the top. But, if you're a Follow Thru/Fact Finder, you'll manage by evaluating appropriate systems. If you're an Implementor/Follow Thru, you'll provide quality control. In neither case will you be likely to initiate innovations, but that doesn't mean you can't encourage the Quick Start talent around you to provide it.

The ideal niche for you puts the "I" before the "deal." You have to place your conative self, your knack, before material gains, prestige, or other considerations. The most profound aspect of conative theory is learning to value inner power more than external glory.

## Sense of Achievement

Conation doesn't define what you can or can't, rather what you will and won't, do.

Any area of interest can incorporate a variety of talents, but some careers cater to your instincts, while others defy you to perform at your best.

One of the great struggles we all go through is protecting our talents from misuse or disuse. Many highly insistent people direct their energies toward protecting the very nature of their conative strength. For instance, many insistent Fact Finders gravitate toward careers in law, where they protect rights or judicially appropriate behavior, or toward education, where they ensure an emphasis on research and facts and figures. Follow Thru insistent people often become involved in planning or systems design to protect security, continuity of services, and adherence to procedures; that's why they make excellent controllers, efficiency experts, and office managers. The Quick Start protects against complacency, against loss of opportunity or denial of options. Therefore a Fact Finder/Quick Start in the labor force might run a union office; if in education, he or she would be pushing for alternative programs.

Having two equally strong modes means going back and forth between them, so that a Quick Start with equal Fact Finder will justify intuitive hunches or self-edit his or her quantity of alternatives to pick the best ones to communicate. A Follow Thru with equal Implementor will categorize everything found in an archeological dig, while a pure Implementor will leave the paperwork to someone else.

The following are examples of how a person within a particular knack will function, and therefore of how you can target your strengths. As you'll see, anyone can deal with change, but a Strategic Planner will need to have new policies justified, a Manufacturer will need to work out changes in space utilization, and a Manager will need to assess the changing options. There are a number of interview techniques, personality tests, and interest inventories that will tell you what a person values, but only the conative connection will predict how good a person will be at doing what he wants to do.

### Fact Finder/Follow Thru: Strategic Planner
*"How does it fit into the system we have?"*
Studies trends
Evaluates sequences
Puts priorities into context
Organizes curriculum
Explains procedures
Justifies policies

### Fact Finder/Quick Start: Manager
*"My hunches are right more than 50 percent of the time."*
Explains bottom line
Calculates risk
Justifies intuition
Specifies challenge
Qualifies sales
Allocates variables
Assesses options

### Fact Finder/Implementor: Technician
*"All that's necessary is this slight adjustment."*
Studies tangibles
Demonstrates probabilities
Allocates space
Evaluates quality
Tests materials
Strategizes protection

### Follow Thru/Fact Finder: Systems Analyst
*"Everything you'd expect is included."*
Structures data
Concentrates on details
Programs specifics
Plans appropriately
Charts probabilities
Concludes thoroughly

### Follow Thru/Quick Start: Program Developer
*"I've planned for every contingency."*
Schedules alternatives
Focuses options
Graphs changes
Designs originals
Sequences diverse elements
Coordinates flexibly
Tracks experiments

### Follow Thru/Implementor: Manufacturer
*"Moving this a couple of feet made all the difference."*
Designs models
Coordinates equipment
Structures manually
Concentrates materials
Patterns work flow
Maintains quality
Plans space

### Quick Start/Fact Finder: Entrepreneur
*"I'll bet I can prove them wrong."*
Challenges status quo
Changes priorities

Revises standards
Improvises presentations
Converts data
Promotes thoroughness

### Quick Start/Follow Thru: Theorist
*"Let's see what happens if we do it a different way."*
Innovates systems
Reforms plans
Reverses trends
Modifies procedures
Originates concepts
Instigates transitions

### Quick Start/Implementor: Pioneer
*"The mountain? Because it's there."*
Competes physically
Challenges endurance
Explores new territory
Alters environment
Defies the elements
Invents

### Implementor/Fact Finder: Mechanic
*"I know just how much force to apply."*
Handles meticulously
Builds precisely
Demonstrates thoroughly
Physically protects established standards
Transports with sophisticated equipment
Makes complex maneuvers

## Implementor/Follow Thru: Quality Controller
*"When I maintain it, it lasts forever."*
Enforces regulations
Guards facilities
Maintains equipment
Designs mechanics
Repairs structures

## Implementor/Quick Start: Adventurer
*"Go ahead and touch it. It won't bite."*
Remodels
Explores
Constructs futuristically
Renders uniquely
Sculpts free-form
Shapes intuitively

### "No Such Thing as Can't"

When I enrolled in Northwestern's Medill School of Journalism, I had made a decision to major in my weakness (both cognitive, as a dyslexic, and conative, since journalism is taught in a Fact Finder manner). In between trying to reform various aspects of student life, I learned how to mimic Fact Finder behavior. When I entered "the real world," I didn't use much of the learned behavior in the ways I was trained, but adapted it to the writing challenges I was forever taking on.

If I recommended pursuing any particular course of study because you matched the dominant MOs in the field, I'd obviously be a hypocrite. Yet that's precisely what most people presume the Kolbe Concept will do. Still, it's much more than a cookie-cutter approach to career planning. It makes you consciously aware of your talents, provides a vocabulary for explaining them, and gives insight into using them. It explains the link between who you are and how you achieve—what the rules are for "playing your own game."

To use your KCI result for career planning, imagine yourself in situations you would enjoy in areas of interest to you, and decide whether you have or could acquire the skills necessary to do it. If you're five feet four, I doubt all the Implementor/Quick Start in the world could make you successful at the basketball slam dunk, so there obviously are physical considerations as well.

With the prerequisite interest and intellectual capacity, your conative capabilities can be utilized so that, for instance, a strategic planner who became a newspaper reporter would look for trends, follow long-term assignments, and develop in-depth expertise in a particular field, while a manager (Fact Finder/Quick Start) would take on exposés, short-term special projects, and challenging investigative pieces. A Follow Thru/Quick Start journalist would report trends, probably do lifestyle features, and give an unusual twist to routine stories.

Can anyone go into retail sales? Sure, but they'll do it differently according to their MO, and have to use varying quantities of energy just to overcome traditional approaches. As you'll find in the next chapter, some specific job requirements would make it unproductive for you even to apply, but that doesn't mean that any field of effort is out of bounds for you.

A retail store clerk with the knack of Quick Start/Implementor would be exceptional demonstrating tangible products—"slicer-dicer" demos would be a classic example. I have a Quick Start niece, resistant in Implementor, who took on such a task only to break the machine before she closed her first sale, but then talked a couple of passersby into seeing if they could get it working—and sold two of the things.

With strength in Follow Thru/Implementor you'd have a person who would design wonderful displays and move products around for the best use of floor space. Though he or she might not bring in a lot of customers, the service orientation would result in long-term satisfaction and repeat business.

Another example—and they could go on through the whole list of knacks—would be the way a Fact Finder/Implementor would keep everything in working order and be able to explain technical products thoroughly enough to satisfy shoppers who arrive with *Consumer Reports* under their arm.

You'll see how employers need to build synergistic teams that mix and match talents, but if you're an individual choosing a career, your MO always offers opportunities for how you *can* do whatever you want to do, not limitations on what you should or shouldn't do.

## Finding the Right Niche for Your Knack

Everyone has a knack. I've asked thousands of people if they have one and never yet have been told "no." But when I ask them to describe this talent, they're often at a loss for words. While we've defined and quantified the differences between gifted and retarded, amiable and aggressive, we've never before had terminology to describe the innate qualities that are both universal and account for the individuality of our capabilities.

Knowing your own MO doesn't guarantee you'll get to use it. Cognitive issues, such as lack of skills or training, can limit opportunities. Affective issues, such as values and attitudes, can also interfere. If those areas do not pose problems, you still have to cope with conative issues:

**1) The rungs of the ladder you have to climb in order to end up in the right niche require the wrong knack:** To become a Fact Finding partner you have to spend years being an efficient Follow Thru employee. To save enough to start your own entrepreneurial Quick Start effort you have to tough it out in Fact Finder middle management jobs in the corporate world.

You can use your strongest modes to "get around" such situations, setting priorities through your Fact Finder that allow you to cope with Follow Thru tasks, or taking work on in the other modes as a Quick Start challenge. However, your tolerance for such conative contrivances will depend upon your degree of motivation.

**2) You're in the right niche but it's the wrong place to stay:** You had the ideal job for your Implementor talents but to move up you have to give it up in favor of a Fact Finder management position. You need the pay increase to feed the family. Or, you are the top Quick Start salesman, so naturally they want to make you the sales manager, who ends up mostly performing the Follow Thru activity of tracking numbers.

Passing up "opportunities" to move up often means

your best bet is to move out. An Implementor job with greater responsibilities or a Quick Start sales position with a larger territory, can make more sense than "up-ward" moves.

**3) You're in the wrong niche but it's all you know how to do:** People often start conversations with me by saying, "If only I'd known about conation sooner . . ." They've already invested thousands of dollars and years of their life training to be a . . . (fill in the blank). They consider themselves stuck.

As long as you have your free will, you're not incapable of solving this dilemma. You can become the person in your field who marches to a different drummer—the Implementor accountant who meets clients in their back rooms and brings someone along to take notes, the Quick Start professor who has more spontaneous activities than lectures and resists giving "normal" assignments.

You can also walk away from the situation, which I've found frequently happens when the lack of satisfaction is not overridden by economic need or offset by outside activities.

**4) You're in the wrong niche, but others are depending on you:** The cry of "We need you. You can't leave us" may be ego-fulfilling, but if you are not fulfilling your personal destiny, the pleas are asking you to sacrifice too much. The most ethical employers will seek opportunities to help you utilize your talents, whether within an organization or through appropriate outplacement. To hold you back because you have the skills is irresponsible management.

Many companies believe they need to retain people in a

job category because of the investment that has been made in specific training. Yet if a worker is not able to perform to capacity because of a conative misfit, neither the company's nor the employee's best interests are being served.

A survey commissioned by the Society of Manufacturing Engineers concluded that the ten best manufacturing companies to work for all "treat their employees, first and foremost, as unique individuals. . . . Employees are expected to participate and contribute, and they are given the intellectual and personal freedom to do so."

You need to consider the contribution you could be making were you fully utilizing your productive capacities. Then break any ties that prevent you from fulfilling that destiny.

**5) You're the wrong sex, age, race, or . . . (fill in the blank) to fill the right niche:** Your MO is ideally suited to being a primary school teacher but you're told that's "not a job for a man." Obviously, there are many other careers for the Follow Thru insistent person (who matches the MO, my data show, for K-3 teachers). But, if that's your choice, the conative connection is now available to you as a way to explain it to others.

I rarely know the sex, age, or race of those filling titles on an organizational chart when I analyze collective KCI results. Often I'll ask why a person with the ideal MO isn't filling a particular job. Frequently it's because no one had ever considered putting them in that spot.

In one case, a Midwestern tool-and-die company had a young woman who spoke up in a seminar to complain that her talents were being squandered in the accounting department. She was bored and about to turn in her resignation. Her MO was exactly what was needed for an assistant marketing position, but, because the accounting clericals had traditionally been female and marketing people were usually male, neither she nor management had considered interviewing her for the position. Within a couple of weeks she had the transfer and has been successful and happy on the job ever since.

You have undoubtedly encountered variations on this theme. You'll be able to recognize them as conative issues if they're predicated on the need to remove obstacles that thwart your natural efforts and to move toward roles that maximize the use of your conative capabilities.

## A Sense of Timing

Time and energy combine in determining your creative output. Through your conative faculty you use time as a dimension of energy. A thought or attitude can be divorced from the context of time, but effort cannot. Effort takes time.

Your MO determines not only your use of time but your sense of time as well, integrating the past, present, and future so that today's efforts use experience to propel you toward your goals.

Your Fact Finder mode is your sense of the past, the ability to put events into historical perspective. "We tried that once and it didn't work." "Based on the evidence we have, this will be worth it." "Until you can prove it, I'm not going to invest the effort." Fact Finder evaluates and allocates both time and energy in the context of experience, and records it so that you take your proper place in the continuum.

The Follow Thru mode is your internal clock. You use it

to sequence events and provide continuity. It is the force that allows you to pace yourself. "We've got to sit down now and plan this out." "There isn't enough time to do all that." "When you've finished what you've started, we'll talk about the next one." Like a personal metronome, Follow Thru sets the rhythm for your efforts and is your ability to integrate past, present, and future.

Your Quick Start mode allows you to predict and deal with events ahead of your time. It helps you to anticipate, to project your imagination into the future, which provides the foresight that helps you deal with change. "We'll never know until we try." "Don't tell me it's never been done. . . . There's always a first time." "I want to see what will happen if . . ."

The Implementor in you keeps you grounded in the present. This here-and-now part of you helps you maintain your footing by providing the foundation or point from which you move in time. The Implementor wants this moment to last and, through that impulse, creates what will endure through time. "When I'm done, no one's ever going to be able to break this." "It captures him perfectly. It's as if he were here." "I want to preserve this place so others can enjoy it as much as we have." It's no coincidence that many environmentalists express their concern for preserving nature by physically demonstrating, like Robert Scott on his expeditions to the North and South poles.

Asking resistant Fact Finders to "wait until all the facts are in" is asking them to put their mind into reverse. They're unlikely to accomplish much in the interim. The same is true if you expect a resistant Follow Thru to "begin as soon as you have the complete picture," or for the resistant Quick Start to "respond immediately," or the resistant Implementor "not to touch it until we're sure how it works." In every case the request is to deny one's own instinct. It results in inactivity or counterproductive behavior.

Give a person with an MO of 6284 all the time he needs to structure a proposal and he'll do nothing with it until the last minute. Ask one with an MO of 5717 to hurry up and he may walk off the job. "If you don't give me the time I need," he might say, "don't expect me to get the job done."

The time people need is determined by their conative instincts—as is the time they give. For an insistent Quick Start to call you while on the run between airplanes means you're a top priority in his or her mind. If an insistent Follow Thru does that to you, you may have barely made the list.

Time-and-motion studies never proved effective because they insinuated that anyone could be trained to fit the parameters of pre-timed and pre-established movement. The Kolbe Concept now explains why some people, when asked to act quickly, will make more mistakes; and others, when required to slow down, will seem to have dulled their senses. Heeding our internal clock is tough when school bells ring every 50 minutes even if you finished the work in ten or needed time to go into more depth, when government and unions "protect" workers with hourly limitations that inhibit all but the Follow Thru's productivity, when time is defined as part of the goal instead of recognized as essential to the process.

"How long did it take you to do that?" you're asked. The best answer is: "All the time I needed."

Your conative self is your most basic reality, the one fixed point in your life. Clearly, what early philosophers identified as the sense of self is inevitably determined by our use of innate talents and results in our sense of achievement. You can take off weight, cover the gray, get remarried, and move to Bora Bora, but what you do there will be in line with what you've always done. If you have an entrepreneurial MO, it won't be long before you're crusading for some change or starting your own beachfront business.

The incredibly high percentage of workers who report stress can be decreased by defining career paths according to natural abilities. Then, if you have to act like a Follow Thru and you aren't one, at the very least you'll know you're finding out how they do it. If no one expects you to become one, you can benefit from the experience of playing the role.

The Stanislavski Method trains actors to dig deep into themselves to recognize the natural actions of a character. You too can plumb the depths of your being to create the image of an insistent anything. You can sustain that role for a while, drawing on every unit of it in your MO. You can carve the turkey in a Follow Thru fashion (evenly cut and delicately placed) because you sense that that's how it's done, or you can attack it Quick Start style (hacking it up) by calling on that energy. You'll do one over the other, depending on who's watching (in-laws usually don't see you wield your Quick Start knife) and on circumstances that cause you to target one mode over another. But your best performance, the one that brings you the greatest sense of accomplishment, not as an actor but as a person, comes with doing what comes naturally.

# – 3 –

# Targeting Mental Energy

I'll call him Hinman, but you'd probably recognize his real name if confidentiality didn't keep me from giving it to you. His rise to stardom had been fast and flashy, and his fall had been just as spectacular. The powerful and highly visible position was gone, and now he was struggling to regain the confidence that had once put him at the top.

"I don't need a shrink," he told me. "I haven't tried to self-destruct or anything. I'm just not able to get back into my game. All I need is a victory or two. That's not a crazy idea. That's reality. I'm told you're pretty damn realistic. So I'll give whatever you're all about a shot."

He'd just arrived in Phoenix, so I suggested he come back to take the KCI the next day, when he wouldn't be tired from traveling. He did, and the results that came out of the computer were exactly as I had expected: they showed neither insistences, resistances, nor a pattern of accommodation.

## Conative Crisis

Under extreme pressure to change or conform at work or at home, some people temporarily lose the ability to express or even recognize their own conative nature. I call this condition conative crisis.

It shows up as a KCI score quite similar to the naturally accommodating scores of the Facilitator, which is why it's essential to have biographical background and a trained person interpreting KCI results.

"Yeah," he said, when I described the implications of his score to him. "Exactly. I haven't been able to be myself for so long I can't remember who I am."

Stress, the kind that builds up inside you and keeps you from doing your best, that prevents you from being productive—that kind of stress is conative, and it comes from trying to perform outside your natural strengths.

According to a survey of the Administrative Management Society, 45 percent of male and 55 percent of female office managers have felt burn-out on their jobs. You can undoubtedly remember times when you've been mentally drained of Implementor energy but the faucet still dripped, when your ability to fix whatever's wrong seems to be in inverse proportion to the amount of effort expended. The tools aren't right. The pipes won't cooperate. That's the feeling of being all thumbs when you've gone beyond the limits of a mode. That's conative crunch, which is the momentary blocking of your ability to succeed.

Or, as you race against a deadline with the clock ticking overhead, there comes a time when you're overwhelmed,

your mind stops functioning creatively, and effort is re-
duced to spinning your wheels. That's the crunch of trying
to force your Quick Start beyond the capacity of your MO.

These short-lived stressful situations are frustrating and
can cause a momentary decrease in self-confidence. But
when you try to live up to false expectations over a long
period, it can become debilitating. The strain can cause
you to lose your sense of self. That's conative crisis.

Since who you are conatively is who you really are,
when you consistently try to operate outside your natural
talents you deny your own worth. If you yield to outside
pressure, try to satisfy unrealistic demands, you may be
able to "pass" some or most of the time, but ultimately
you'll fail. No one can mask the conative self indefinitely
without destroying his inner drive. When you push yourself to your conative limits, you begin to spin your wheels,
trying to perform with intensities that are not natural for
you. Your productivity slackens. You become nonfunctional.

"I've been pushed and shoved and battered and
bruised," Hinman went on. "They wanted me to be a little
more of this and a lot more of that. They sent me off to
places that taught me how to handle the media, how to
dress right, they even had my hair 'styled.'

"I did whatever the hell they wanted me to do because
it was all very exciting. And for a while it even worked—
I thought. I was the bright light of the place. I was making
it big. My timing was perfect—until they taught me how
to forget everything I knew how to do. When I woke up
and realized what was wrong, that I couldn't function
anymore, they told me I'd lost my nerve. The problem is
I'd been right in the first place and should never have

given in. I let people coming up from behind push me out in front of a steam roller. I don't know if they were doing it on purpose, but they danced on my grave."

Not knowing your own mind is one reason for getting into stressful situations. Most of what you do is based on expectations—yours or others. If you expect yourself to be able to work under deadline pressure and don't have much Quick Start, you're setting yourself up for a fall.

It was interesting to learn that even Hinman's meteoric rise, which had been written about in the press, was actually a distortion from the very beginning. He was in the right place at the right time because he had very deliberately placed himself there.

He and his wife both described how he had developed strategies, clipped articles, catalogued examples, and built a case for himself that determined his calculated plan of attack. He knew the stumbling blocks, where all the mines were placed in all the fields of battle.

When I began to describe the characteristics of the Follow Thru/Fact Finder approach, his wife nodded eagerly. "You're talking about how he used to act. That's it. It was always comfortable for me because I guess I'm a lot like that, too. But all of a sudden it was as if he turned his back on himself." She looked at him and said, "I guess you thought you had to be like all those people around you who really were more the Quick Start types Kathy describes. That was never you. You weren't like that. I'm almost glad it didn't work when you tried it, because I love the real you."

When Hinman left my office it was with an assignment. He promised to send me a five-year-plan for himself, to clip articles about people in the limelight who function much as he would when left to himself. He was going to reorganize his life and get back to the constants that meant most to him. He'd assess what he needed to do to put his conative house back in order.

He sent me materials on a regular basis until it was clear he was incorporating them into his everyday functioning. About eighteen months later, I called him and said I thought the last interview I'd read about him showed that he was right on target. He was on the rise once again, and he was recommending that people follow their own inclinations and resist any pressure to do otherwise. The only place I faulted him was for suggesting in those interviews that everyone develop long-range plans for themselves. "What worked for you isn't going to be the conative solution for everyone," I reminded him. "The point is for each of us to do it in our own distinctive way."

Another client of mine, a property development firm, promoted one of its best shopping center managers to a management position in the home office. Overseeing all the property managers in his firm, he found his role—and his life—had changed. Much like the case of an instinctive Quick Start salesman moved into a sales manager slot, his job MO went from a promoter profile with lots of Quick Start to one requiring mostly Fact Finder and Follow Thru. He had fit the bill initially with an MO of 3395. Now I was talking to him as he sat behind a big desk in a high-rise office building. He wasn't able to make good use of his Quick Start talent, nor was he accommodating his Implementor need to be out and about. He had the stress of a man painted into a very tight corner.

"But I can't turn my back on the salary," he told me. "The benefits, the prestige. I can't go back. If I do, it looks like I failed."

"But how can you turn your back on your own instincts?" I said. "Are you enjoying 'the benefits?' Is this really what you'd call a step forward?"

I asked him to describe for me how he felt as he drove to work in the mornings.

"I dread the trip," he told me, "because I know when I get there I'll be too busy with details to accomplish anything significant. The things I do all day don't bring me satisfaction. I know just how empty I'll be feeling when I go back home at night."

We talked of times when he'd felt energetic, when he'd thrived on working long hours and solving tough problems. "I suppose I looked like a Type A person," he said. "Everyone said I ought to slow down and enjoy life a little. But that's when I was at the top of my game. I was having a ball. Now I'm acting like a damned Type B and I'm stressed out by the behind-the-desk stuff."

He paused and looked out his window a long moment. "You've given me a challenge," he said. "I'm not quite sure what I'll do with it."

Within a couple of weeks he called my office to tell me he had submitted his resignation and had been reinstated in his old role. "The minute I decided to do it I felt better. It's like a huge weight has been lifted from my shoulders."

His boss had sat in on one of our presentations, so he understood the rationale behind the move. But the commitment the man had made to himself didn't require that anyone else understand, just that they give him the room to perform through his natural strengths.

When we did a seminar a few weeks later for his peer property managers, they commented on what a difference his return to character had made. As one of them said, "I'm sure he wakes up every morning thankful that he had the guts to do it. I admire a man who knows his own mind that well."

You won't accomplish much if you strive against your instincts, forcing action contrary to your natural impulse, but you'll end up exerting just as much or more energy in the effort. Since mental energy is a limited resource, your 20 units can be frittered away, as you pile up work you'll never tackle, design systems to which you'll never adhere, and gather data you'll never read.

I started a speech to a group of prospective small business owners by saying something to the effect of this: "You're taking a big risk if you're going to be putting most of what you own into this business. You're going to have to put yourself on the line—your reputation, money, time, and energy. You'll give up much of your social life because there simply won't be time for everything and your business will have to come first. You'll be at odds with local government, state government, and federal government; all of which demand an incredible amount of paperwork and have taken away most of the economic incentives for small businesses. What you need from suppliers will arrive late and be faulty. Your employees will consider you the big-bad-boss, and many of your efforts to make them "like family" will backfire in your face. The bonuses you offer will never replace the security they seek, and you won't be able to afford other benefits that match the offers they threaten to take. Your banker will ask for projections you know are wish-lists, and you'll feel you're living on the edge even when profits are rolling in. Your accountant will say "can't" when what you asked was "how?" Your attorney will always seem to understand the other side better than he will what you're trying to do. Your family will ask when the great rewards you promised are going to be available. But you know everything has to stay in the business if you're going to keep growing. They're ready and waiting for you to show up in time for dinner, vacations, and holidays, but you're never quite finished with what you have to do. Everything centers on making this work, yet all the odds are against it. Why? Why would you ever get yourself into this?

"If what I've said discourages you, please quit taking notes and assessing the value of having to sit through a speech like this. Go and get a job or stay with the security you already have. If what I've said makes you want to come out fighting, to prove you can beat the system, succeed in spite of all this—go for it!"

The chairman of the event asked how dare I (I'm used to that expression) say such discouraging things to the future business owners of America, but at least a dozen people wrote or called to say, "Thanks, I needed that"—in essence, telling me they had had doubts but just hadn't known why. Some others came up with fire in their eyes saying things like, "If that's what it takes, that's what I'm willing to give." I always felt more convinced if I sensed what they also wanted to add was, "Nothing can stop me from going for it!" If I've helped people target their mental energy—make commitments—I feel I've helped them get to first base.

A similar kind of speech could be given to those entering the corporate rat race. It would center on the necessary strategies, the way the game has to be played appropriately, the diplomacy it requires, the observation of every detail along the way. That presentation would find the Quick Start wanting to hightail it out of there and the Fact Finder's juices flowing.

Of course the same "harsh reality" tactic could work with the Follow Thru who applauds the systems inherent in one situation over another, or with the Implementor who would self-select the hands-on world, while those resistant to strenuous physical environments would run the other way. Describing opportunities in rigorously challenging terms is one of the best ways to separate the conative realities from your wishful thinking.

An entrepreneur whose business took off rapidly soared in the start-up years. But she did a personal nosedive when the business outgrew her Quick Start strengths and needed more Fact Finder than she could muster. Instead of turning day-to-day operations over to someone with the necessary strengths, she tried to learn how to be a management-by-objectives type herself. But all the management training in the world couldn't change who she was. It simply made her tentative about her own talents. She reined in her Quick Start zeal for developing innovative products and new business connections while beating her head against the finite limit of her Fact Finder talents. By denying her own strengths, she proved what is so often true of Quick Starts—she made rags-to-riches a round trip.

Quick Starts I've interviewed suffer from the fear that they'll never repeat successes because they may not have enough Fact Finder to be able to justify their intuition. Such people often believe they "bluffed" their way through school. They usually crammed and waited until the last minute to do papers—the same way they're succeeding now, by not following traditional paths or staying within the lines.

One man I worked with had tried to cloak himself in entrepreneurial garb, but it never fit. An Implementor insistent craftsman, he created a process that was a technical advance in molding plastic. He didn't want to sell the patent to the mass producer corporations who wouldn't stick to the quality which is so important to the Implementor mind, so he decided to take on those roles himself. By the time he came to me he had been out of his element for years, searching for a way to promote his own invention.

He had started and closed down a manufacturing operation. "I made the first few and then tried to turn it over to employees but they just didn't get it. They tried short cuts and all that, but I didn't need that kind of help."

As he turned further away from his natural bent and the work that had been fulfilling for him, moving instead toward managing and selling, he suffered greater and greater stress. "I've been in meetings with potential buyers for so long I can't remember why the thing worked in the first place."

It was no surprise when his KCI result showed conative crisis. He had been struggling against his own instincts— a battle no one can win. But what had seemed an endless downward spiral stopped when quantified in conative terms. Understanding the problem helped him attack it head-on. He went back to a hardware business that had fed his conative needs, and after six months his KCI results were back to his natural MO of 4637. He was also hard at work designing a model for a do-it-yourself sprinkler system.

People suffering conative malfunctioning are often lumped together with those who are emotionally disturbed. Some medical and psychological journals list afunctional or dysfunctional problems as conative, using the term yet not explaining it. But nowhere have I found prescriptive approaches that are conative.

If you are having a problem getting things done, the solutions need to address conative causes and effects. Conative crisis that has gone on for more than a few weeks can make it difficult if not impossible for you to remain in touch with your natural intentions. You've masked your instincts even from yourself. At that point, it is essential to recall those times when you felt a sense of accomplishment. It may mean going back to junior high school—when you played in the band or did such a great job on the science project. Those episodes people describe to me as the great moments of their lives are the ones I look to for clues to their internal drive. I find that people come out of conative crisis within a few weeks of first identifying the problem and locating the causes. More often than not, the cause is trying to satisfy another person's expectations.

## Crisis or Opportunity?

Your MO remains constant throughout your life. The adult whose best efforts are spontaneous actions and off-the-top-of-the-head responses was the child who got into everything and insisted on doing things without being shown. There are stages in life, however, when the conative self comes into question.

My data shows that the two stages of life with the highest incidence of conative crisis are midlife and the teenage years. Approximately 5 percent of employed people's KCI results indicate conative crisis, while 15 percent of those between the ages of 14 and 19 and between 40 and 50 fall into that category. Mid-life crisis and teenage angst are symptoms of severe conative strain. The other situations that most increase the probability of conative crisis are being a housewife and retirement.

In our society, few teens have had the opportunity for self-discovery. They have been told what to do and how to act by a school system that enforces particular modes of achievement. Their responsibilities at home, if they have any, are often merely what is considered appropriate for their age and sex, rather than for their talents. Perhaps fifteen-year-old Josh has the best eye for design in the family, but does he get a chance to suggest what would look good in the living room? Probably not; it's not his "place"—the 5852 is out cutting the grass. His will is being thwarted and his contribution denied. Why wouldn't he rebel?

The routines of teens are out of sync with who they are. Sometimes school activities can capture individual talents and bring together a community of kids to put on a show or put out a newspaper or such. These outside activities can prove the training ground for their use of talent, a place where they can discover their innate abilities and their need for team effort. Is it any wonder former football days are relived so often?

When teenagers are working to contribute to the family welfare or volunteering effort for community needs, they have a sense of purpose. But many teens have nothing to provide them with self-esteem. Doing what they are told is not satisfying their inner self. "Hanging out" is purposeless. This unrealistic betwixt-and-between stage is a breeding time for conative crisis. It puts a strain on the youngsters going through it and a society that has institutionalized it.

Middle age can bring with it its own conative crises. The 45-year-old may finally recognize that the pain of not functioning as his or her natural self is not worth the price. If that most fundamental form of success—the freedom to be yourself—has not been achieved, the very sense of being is in a state of confusion. When denial of self has been the pattern, breaking out of it is both jarring and rewarding. The executive who becomes a beach bum may be an unfulfilled Implementor trying to regain his sense of the physical space around him. The Fact Finder civic volunteer may go back to school to satisfy a need for more information grounded in the academic perspective.

The housewife who tries to meet everyone else's needs may lose her sense of self in the process. How can she be enough of a Follow Thru to keep everyone on schedule, plan meals, and maintain an efficient house, and also be flexible enough to deal with every crisis that comes up, adjusting her life according to the myriad changes wrought by a busy husband and active children? How can she be enough of an Implementor to be a capable mender, repairer, gardener, and transporter of little people and big projects, and be expected as well to always have her priorities established, be well read, and be a good manager of finances and all the family resources?

She won't be able to live up to such expectations, whether self- or externally imposed. Her true imperatives, her needs for self-expression, get lost in the shuffle. Add in the expectation that she care for an elderly parent and she'll be completely submerged.

Retirement—and the aging process itself—is often frought with conative frustrations. Just as we tend to stereotype all toddlers as needing Implementor activity and then expect them to turn into Fact Finders as school children, so we tend to characterize retirees as being satisfied out on the golf course, causing us to offer mostly Implementor crafts for senior citizen recreation.

Physical limitations may alter the ways in which we can act on our conative instincts. A Fact Finder insistent person may not have the visual acuity to see detail or the hearing necessary to judge auditorially. Perhaps she'll ask seemingly incessant questions, attempting to fill the information void. The insistent Follow Thru has always needed control over his schedule and plan of action. When others assume that responsibility, even if he is infirm, he suffers a loss of identity and may become disoriented in his self-expectations. Retirement, at first, may seem a relief from years of effort, but not replacing income-generating effort with some conatively-suited activity robs a person of a sense of accomplishment and erodes self-respect.

The process of reaffirmation is well worth the struggle. I often remind people going through any of these periods that the Chinese character for "crisis" is much the same as the one for "opportunity."

## Conative Crunch

Any kind of stress is obviously a problem. But you can work despite emotional stress; in fact, some people's creativity soars in periods of personal trauma. It can cause them to avoid the affective and concentrate on the doing domain. Functioning becomes a problem, however, when we try to force our conative mode beyond its natural limit. And one of the locales where this most often takes place is the office.

"I think you'd better talk with Helen," my secretary said. "She doesn't even remember getting the materials." Strange. Everyone can always count on Helen. She's the ultimate administrative assistant, always able to get you what you want when you want it, always on top of things. A perfect fit with her job, her Facilitator talent is put to constant use. She's the one person I'm always confident will have handled preparations. But today she looked like a *Cathy* cartoon as she glanced a little wildly around the office, uncertain what to do first, her lipstick chewed off, her normally sleek hair in total disarray.

"What's the problem?" I asked her.

"You wouldn't believe what's being expected of me. We're going through a conversion of our phone system. Everything around me is torn up, the lines all ring at once, I can't get through to the people I need to reach. In the midst of that everyone on this floor is either out of town or about to go out of town, so nothing is getting decided. I'm trying to satisfy everyone's need to get answers, so I'm running all around the place—and then get back to my desk and find long-distance messages from people I've been trying to get answers from for days. I can't do my job under these conditions. It's just plain impossible."

Helen was feeling the stress of a conative crunch, which many of us go through several times a day. The key is recharging your mental batteries so you don't get stuck.

"Sounds horrible," I said. "Since you can't be productive under those conditions, why don't you ask Tom if he'd mind if you took the rest of the day to review upcoming projects. Take the files you need to a conference room, or to a park, and settle in for the afternoon."

As a matter of fact, her boss wished he'd thought of that himself. Better to have the switchboard take the calls for awhile. He couldn't afford to have Helen dysfunctional.

It didn't even take the rest of the day for her to recuperate. She'd just needed mental space. As a Facilitator, she would not insist on facts or plans or taking on the chaos as a challenge or yanking the phone cords out herself, but she was vulnerable to her own kind of burnout—a kind of accommodation overload that left her with nowhere to go. It was not her nature to insist, or to resist any way that people needed her to work, and now she was paralyzed.

Repeated efforts that don't help reach goals or fulfill conative commitments are the cause of conative crunch. They create a dilemma rather than satisfying a need. Conation is goal-directed behavior, so the thwarting of the goal diminishes its effectiveness. By removing herself from the situation long enough to regain her centering point, Helen went back to her desk able to once again accommodate the situation.

"Thanks, I needed that," she said when she called the next day. "I simply decided to hold my ground. I went back in there and explained to the installers that my phone *would* be operating correctly by the end of the day because the whole place revolves around it as a communications center. I'd never realized how key I was to this place. The one thing I'm going to insist on as an accommodating person is being able to accommodate!"

Thank goodness Helen wasn't misguided into thinking a seminar on assertiveness was in order. Learning to use insistences and resistances wisely is one thing. Trying to make a Facilitator anything else is downright immoral— and counterproductive. "Assertiveness training" can confuse attitude with actions. Asserting your conative self is essential, but it doesn't require being an aggressor. And self-confidence comes with doing things through your strengths, not following an all-purpose formula.

Helen's mental batteries were recharged by her recognizing her own distinctive contribution. Since we're motivated to act in the first place by the cognitive and affective, it makes sense that we get re-invigorated the same way. Lack of appreciation for your efforts, whether from others or by yourself can be de-energizing. Feeling unneeded can make you ineffective, no matter how conatively suited you are to what you're doing.

The most effective compliments are for efforts made through natural talents. Had Tom told Helen she was terrific in the crisis she would have felt it false praise. She knew she wasn't operating like a Quick Start. When he thanked her for trying to be flexible, she could accept it as genuine. When he teased her about accommodating the enemy by giving the installers cookies off her desk, they could both laugh. Recognition for her real abilities helped her know they were accepted and appreciated.

Management trainees in these enlightened times are frequently reminded to compliment workers, to be generous with praise and cautious with criticism. It's a fine idea. We all do like compliments, and you do get more flies with honey, and so on. But be sure you praise wisely and knowledgeably.

A month after Liz went to work for a top ad agency, she called me in consternation. Her boss was very pleased. She complimented Liz repeatedly on her punctuality, her organization, her planning. Liz, however, is a 4 in Follow Thru. Yes, she was pulling out every smidge of Follow Thru to make the right impression in a new environment. What she wanted, though, was a word of praise for her originality, for her quick reactions under pressure, for her innovative scheduling. If the boss was pleased with Liz's Follow Thru, she would very likely be *displeased* when it ran out, as it surely would in a major crisis. On the other hand, if she appreciated Liz's Quick Start, she'd consider overlooking an occasional lapse in punctuality. Liz was feeling very insecure.

I didn't know the woman she worked for, so I couldn't help directly, but I told her what I suspected: that her boss *knew* how difficult Follow Thru work was for her and was therefore praising her efforts in that area. It's a common mistake. Sometimes people make it with their children. Praise them for something that isn't a strong suit and it's almost as if you were wishing they were someone else.

Richard knew he could make a difference and cared greatly about the work he was doing. All it would take were a few more days and he'd have the books completely converted to the new computer system. He was an 8 in Fact Finder and knew exactly how significant the benefits would be. It was worth the units of Follow Thru he had to give to the project.

Trouble was, Richard only had 5 units of Follow Thru to give, and the conversion had taken all of that and still needed more. The tediousness of it was more than he could take.

"My mind is fried," Richard announced. "I feel like one of those little characters in Pac Man, the smiley little faces that get zapped by the monsters. Every time I start to work on the computer, *whap*! a blue monster swallows me. I couldn't even sort my socks right now, let alone all the data going into this thing. I need to just vegetate for awhile."

Computers may substitute for or assist our cognitive brains. Maybe they *can* think. But they require input. They have no conation.

Computers will never replace people because they can't take initiative. That's the conative dimension that only living things can contribute.

Richard's burnout was a symptom of conative stress. He had used up his Follow Thru without being able to replenish it. He was finding it impossible to fulfill his commitment to the project.

Normal conative fatigue, even without success, can be rejuvenated after sleep and with leisure. A little downtime and Richard would usually be ready to go back at it. But, when he'd been working against his grain for so long, rest no longer helped. The demands he was making of himself left him inadequate leisure and no time for recreational outlets. The more he had tried, the worse it had become.

The conative mind can't sustain long periods of stress

or conflict. It just plain stops functioning. Ideas may go round and round in the cognitive part of your brain, but you won't act on them. You may feel terrible, but you won't do anything about it. It's not worth it when it doesn't lead to accomplishment. You'll just quit trying. Sometimes you have days like that. If they turned into weeks or even months you'd become incapacitated.

Richard stopped the downward spiral by dealing with its causes. He knew his KCI result didn't match what he'd been trying to do, so he finally stepped back and looked for other ways to accomplish the goal.

The first step in solving conative dilemmas is always to seek others who can inject the mode in which you're deficient. But since there were no funds to hire a Follow Thru programmer, Richard didn't have the alternative of getting someone else in on the project. He had to depend on himself.

He tried the next-best alternative. He switched into his Quick Start mode to look for short-cuts and for ways around problems. He discovered trial-and-error solutions that weren't in the manuals. His Fact Finder clicked in when he got on the phone and sought information from the manufacturer. He found he could accomplish much of what he'd been unsuccessfully trying to do by substituting his still functional capacities.

Short-term conative deficits are usually in a particular mode or two. Getting yourself out of that rut and into more productive methods is the solution to such situational stress.

Lethargy is short-lived if you deal day in, day out with ways of dodging further overdrafts. If the problem is not having the Follow Thru energy to help your kids with their homework, you can justify it through your Fact Finder as being their work, not yours. If there's no Fact Finder brain power for figuring out a fiftieth-anniversary gift for the folks, you can call your Quick Start sister who usually has clever ideas.

Bypassing conative stress by bringing in outside help is one of the benefits of having partners, living near an extended family, or playing on any team.

## Switching Your Mental Gears

When you're totally on your own, whether in a work situation or personally, you can fall into the trap of trying to put out the same energy, finding it harder and harder to stop the plummeting energy level. Loneliness can be caused by many factors, but it often leads to conative problems. Even when there are others around, it may be that no one in the room understands how you need to do things or why you resist their way, but at least you have someone to bail you out in a crunch. People who have no one to turn to are most likely to suffer conative burn-out. They try to do it all.

A friend of mine was a political lobbyist with an MO of 7652. He spent most of his life—and his Fact Finder energies—testifying before committees and drafting legislation for his largely Fact Finder clientele. But even a 7 in Fact Finder is a limited resource, and getting the job done required that he still keep going each day, even when the usual resources were used up. His job also demanded and consumed all of his Quick Start flexibility, and his Implementor was expended traveling. To stretch for those extra productive hours each day, all that was left was Follow Thru.

When everything else was spent, he could kick into a Follow Thru mode by surrendering the detail of such activities as writing and vote-counting, and turn to issues of overall structure. He would pull out the flow chart and start tracing legislative activity in terms of structural trends.

If you've ever done any writing—and term papers in high school count, too—you've probably discovered this kind of gear-switching on your own. You inch along, burrowing deeper and deeper in the Fact Finder mode until you need to come up for air. You've dug a nice hole for yourself and you can't go any further on this detailed level, but you find your energy renewed for an extra hour's worth of effort simply by backing off and looking at the big picture—the Follow Thru structure. But even that extra energy is expended after a while, and the report is still due tomorrow, so you decide to just wing it for a while, typing, without editing, to discover what's on your mind: the Quick Start approach. When you're really stumped and you still have to go on, that's when you start laying out the three-by-five notecards and moving them around—an Implementor manipulation of physical representations of your ideas.

Many people begin the writing process from a Fact Finder perspective not because it's their forte, but because they were taught to write by teachers with that bias. Having given the KCI to hundreds of educators, I've found Fact Finders dominate the profession from junior high to university classrooms. In primary grades it's Follow Thru teachers who encourage us to come up with a complete outline before we begin.

Yet no matter what we were taught, some of us start writing by dumping our minds out first and later going back to fill in detail. Those of us who are resistant in Fact Finder and still find ourselves functioning as authors have to unlearn the process we were taught, break the rules, and trust our ability to draw on other talents. Success in any endeavor depends on calling upon our strengths— even when it makes us look like we're bucking the system.

Our minds are like kids who need to be kept busy on a long, rainy day. A particular activity will hold off restlessness for only so long. We burn out in any one mode. Mental discipline becomes a problem when we try to force any one mode beyond its natural limit.

A Follow Thru advertising designer always needed closure that just wasn't going to be there. The solution for her was to kick into a Fact Finder mode and set priorities for which aspects of her work might offer "little closures." The big picture never was going to be truly wrapped up. She had to find smaller units with which she could cope.

Any Follow Thru beset with a chaotic situation can draw on that energy to find the pattern within the pattern, even if the pattern consists mostly of exceptions. Identifying the structure as such will be reassuring.

Gear-switching is what allows a sales rep to make those extra calls at the end of the day when all her Quick Start energy is gone. She can appeal to her Fact Finder instincts: "I get a positive response for one out of every ten calls. I need three more to make my ten, so let's go." Or the appeal to Implementor: "Take the walk." Or through Follow Thru: "I need closure—one more call will round out this part of town."

People biased toward a particular mode teach problem solving by saying you *must* study books on the subject to see how it's been done in the past (Fact Finder), or learn the theory or formula for it (Follow Thru), or experiment with radical "whack on the side of the head" innovations (Quick Start), or work with models (Implementor).

The truth is that there is no one "right" way—it's situational.

To switch into Fact Finder, ask "What is the number one thing I'm trying to accomplish?"
To switch into Follow Thru, ask "How will I know when I'm done?"
To switch into Quick Start, ask "What is the exception?"
To switch into Implementor, ask "How can I show it?"

When you've used up your mental energy in a particular mode, you have no more of it to give until you recharge your batteries. If you keep trying to make lists of what you need to do even though you've drained all your Follow Thru, you'll just lose the list anyway. You're simply adding stress to the equation by berating yourself.

### Situational Stress

In considering situations in which you have had stress, try matching your expectations with what you guess your own conative makeup to be. This obviously requires knowing your own mind. One way to discover just who you are conatively, even without taking the KCI, is to track the types of activities that cause you stress.

If stress comes from not having enough appropriate information, having your quest for specificity and clarification inhibited, you probably have a lot of Fact Finder.

If stress comes from lack of closure, from not having a sense of completion, too many unfinished projects, and not enough routine or structure to your life, you have a lot of Follow Thru.

If stress comes from being held back, from not having enough challenges, not being able to take risks and heed your sense of adventure, and not being able to act intuitively, you have a lot of Quick Start.

If stress is being physically confined, not having the freedom to work with your hands, not having the quality tools to work with, or having to lend those you have to others, you have a lot of Implementor.

Along with the stress of being blocked in the use of energy through an insistent mode, there is also the stress of trying to act through a mode in which you are resistant.

Having to justify your actions, establish priorities or do things in great detail is stress for those resistant to Fact Finder.

Having to stay within regulations, follow procedures or plan ahead, is stress for those resistant to Follow Thru.

Having to wing it, act spontaneously, play hunches or ad lib, is stress for those resistant to Quick Start.

Having to physically produce a result by making, building or fixing tangible things, is stress for those resistant to Implementor.

Any mode in which you are accommodating is one through which you can act without stress, so long as the degree to which you will use the mode does not exaggerate your capacity in that mode. Expectations have to match the realities of your MO.

## Managing Mental Energy

Whenever I consult with a client organization, the first thing I do is have everyone from senior management on down take the KCI. I also have them complete another instrument we call the Job-KCI. The Job-KCI is designed to give a picture of what it takes to get a job done, or, more accurately, several pictures. One comes from the point of view of management. When a supervisor takes the Job-KCI, the results spell out his or her *requirements* for how the job is to be handled. A different perspective may come from the employee. If you were to take the Job-KCI for your own job, the results would portray your *self-expectations*. They would show just how much of each mode you think it takes to succeed in your role.

Your peers and subordinates can also take Job-KCIs to tell you how they see your job. A person working for you might count on you to react in certain ways, but may never have been able to articulate why. The Job-KCI removes judgments of good or bad, smart or dumb, and focuses on requirements and expectations that haven't been spelled out on job descriptions, but can nevertheless determine whether you succeed or fail.

"I knew there was a reason Susan was so good in that job," one boss said, "but I never would have figured out that it's because she can prioritize all the options. Yet that's what's made her shine, now that I think of it."

I find that the conative makeup of managers can bias what they think they need in a job. They often want people to follow their example—or worse yet, to be 10's in everything. By seeing their expectations in chart form, they become more objective. When I highlight every name on the organizational chart in bright colors according to each individual's dominant Action Mode, the slots filled by those with Fact Finder dominance show up in Orange, Follow Thru in Blue, Quick Start in Green, and Implementor in Yellow. I do the same with resistances and then, on the same type of chart, compare the colors of the talents from the KCIs with the expectations and requirements shown on the Job-KCIs. When I hold these charts up in front of everyone, the reaction, often enough, is for them to gasp. You'd gasp too if you suddenly discovered that the team responsible for new technology was constitutionally resistant to change, or that the person doing the scheduling doesn't by nature plan ahead.

Businesses have to cope with limitless issues involving ethics or personalities or lack of fundamental skills, but deep down, most work-related problems are conative. A clash of colors on the organizational chart means a clash of wills, and no amount of kindness or good intentions or time management seminars or assertiveness training is going to completely neutralize that. A flash of color where it's not expected can mean people struggling against themselves or against the work at hand. A monochromatic chart means that certain types of drive are missing, that the conative mix is too uniform to produce the synergistic effect of well-managed diversity. The presence of such conative problems invariably pinpoints the cause of lost productivity. Companies with these indicators usually know a problem exists, but they haven't had a way to identify or effectively correct it.

The seven-member policy committee of a client company asked me to help evaluate candidates for a difficult-to-fill management position. "We've tried several types of people in it, but no one seems to be quite right," I was told. When the seven members of the committee completed the Job-KCI, the reason for their problem became quite clear. No three of the group agreed on the requirements for the job. Two of them expected the manager to be a by-the-book Fact Finder who would act on experience and only take calculated risks. Two believed the role required more of a technical background, a combination of Fact Finder and Implementor talent for the tangible. Two others' Job-KCI indicated a strong insistence on a person with a sense of urgency, a Quick Start who would stick his or her neck out and deal with the immediacy of the company's need to become more pioneering in their industry. The seventh vote was for a Facilitator who could manage the multitude of strong-willed characters already on board.

It took three hours of intense discussion, but the policy committee finally reached the consensus that the Fact Finder/Quick Start already in the role was best suited to continue. And now she had the support necessary to do the job her way.

## Strain, Conflict, and Tension

There are three types of conative stress that I have been able to identify and quantify through my research: strain, conflict, and tension.

**Strain:** *Strain* is self-inflicted. It's caused by trying to "improve" in the Action Modes in which you are naturally resistant. Or trying to deny your own creative bent. It comes with trying to emulate someone conatively different from you, or yielding to pressure to be someone other than who you are. It can be as dangerous to your well-being as a blood transfusion of a mismatched natural type. It can keep you from fulfilling your natural destiny.

You may admire the way Martha works nights to put herself through graduate school, but if you put your energies toward completing the same Fact Finder course you couldn't satisfy your Quick Start need for exploring other options. The entire family may hold her up as a role model but you may do best to wish her well as you go down a different path.

You may want to win your father-in-law's approval by repairing your own carburetor, but it'll only put more strain on you when you have to explain why it still isn't working. Strain in the workplace comes with trying to become what the boss or job requires, mimicking the wrong conative role model, or trying to fit others' expectations. You may recognize that people around you are tired of your changing your mind all the time, but if you try to control the impulse to originate new ways, you'll suffer strain.

When a resistant Follow Thru takes it upon himself to establish procedures and enforce regulations, or a resistant Quick Start puts pressure on herself to meet multiple deadlines, they are wasting time and energy. Both are putting themselves under strain.

It's just as counterproductive to try *not* to be something you instinctively are. An insistent Quick Start reining in his instincts and sticking to yesterday's decision is causing himself strain. The Fact Finder denying her need to decide based on thoroughly defined options suffers such strain that the decision to go along brings little pleasure, even if it turns out to be a good one. The Fact Finder, making money on a chancy investment, might call it dumb luck, but hopes never to go through such strain again.

Unlike someone in conative crisis, a person suffering the stress of working against his grain knows exactly who he is conatively, but also recognizes that's not how he's going to succeed in a particular situation. An intern in a hospital sensed his forte as a Fact Finder diagnostician, yet he was undergoing the strain of Follow Thru/Implementor duty. The system of medical education requires this initiation, even if it's neither maximizing the use of his talents nor helping him avoid mounting stress.

The rites of passage into most jobs require working under strain, even though there are often entry-level tasks that could be assigned according to talents. As long as the individual maintains a sense of self, it's possible to survive such periods of strain—even to benefit from them. They are lessons in empathy, in understanding what it takes to work in surgery or in the emergency room or as a lab technician—even if what you'll become is a psychiatrist.

We *can* do anything that's required, so long as there's

light at the end of the tunnel. But a secretary with an MO of 3296 *needed* to get out of a job she knew took 6833. Her KCI and her Job-KCI weren't telling her anything she didn't already know. The strain was obvious to her. It's just that she had confused it with emotional stress and thought she could control it over time.

"I just thought I had an attitude problem. I wanted things that weren't available to me and was bitter about my lack of a college degree, for instance," she told me. In fact, a degree wasn't what was stopping her—all she needed was a chance to prove herself in a job that used her sales and promotional abilities.

*To remove strain, stop doing what you're doing.* That may mean doing nothing for a period of time so that in the conative silence you can re-establish your centering point, your sense of purpose. Knowing your conative strengths and stress points allows you to be self-directed and goal-oriented, and to cope with the consequences of your own actions. As imperfect creatures who fall short of a 10 in every talent, we cannot accomplish all things without a community of effort. To avoid strain, recognize that your need for help is balanced by your ability to give assistance. Rather than suffer the strain of self-reliance or a senseless effort to modify actions, you can accept responsibility for using your talents well, and take pride in the accomplishments they bring.

People often have to sacrifice economic security and even the wrath of others to gain their conative freedom, and ultimately many make the choice to withstand the strain in order to provide security for their families or such things as prestige for themselves. I have never, however, talked with a person at the end of his or her career who thought the sacrifice had been worth it. "If I had it to do all over again . . ." they would have done as the country-western song says, and told their bosses to "take this job and shove it."

**Conflict:** "I don't get it. Why can't you just do it the way I showed you? Now you've gone and destroyed the whole system I set up. We'll have to go back and start all over," Murray told his co-worker.

"No, we don't," Dale replied. "The short cut I've discovered will just make it that much easier."

"Sure. Easier for you," Murray said. "The corners you cut create twice the work for me. I've got to go back and be sure nothing you did destroys the functioning of the whole project."

The conflict between these two is not only determined by their strongest modes, but by their resistances. There will be stress between people working directly with one another if they have a difference of 4 or more in any mode. Even if Murray understands why Dale functions more through Quick Start, it will not totally mitigate the conflict. "I don't care if you're a damn Quick Start," Murray might say, "I won't let this project go down the tubes just because you needed to experiment with some cockamamie alternative. Do your 'creative' stuff on your own time."

It's amazing how creativity gets a bad name in resistant Quick Start environments just because people haven't recognized that creative contribution can come through any mode. Whatever the pejoritive affixed to the Mode of your greatest resistance ("picayune" Fact Finder, "obsessive" Follow Thru, "obstructionist" Quick Start, "yup 'n' nope"

Implementor), the use of it shows the affective overlay that often comes with conative conflict. We haven't recognized that natural wills and won'ts aren't conspiracies or attempts to put down another's efforts.

Synergy requires that conative differences be at hand, yet, without an understanding of the causes of conflict, great effort has been devoted to removing such differences rather than building on them. Training programs, even marriage counseling, have emphasized how people working together need to adopt rather than adapt to each other's methods of operation. Conforming to "the way it's done" insinuates a right and wrong or a struggle for one MO to dominate another. It never has worked and never will work to match anybody to a way of doing anything. Such is the stuff of rebellion, for no person can ever impose his or her will on another's.

*Conflict* is unavoidable. It stems from the same causes as synergy—vast differences in the way people get things done. By surrounding yourself with your conative clones you can artificially remove conflict, but you'll replace it with inertia. Nature has provided us with a natural distribution of each mode in the general population. It is this balance in nature that provides diversity, yet the existence in everyone of some of each instinct makes universal the spirit within us. Recognizing each instinct within yourself enables you to empathize with its presence in others.

The issue with conflict is not to lessen it but to manage it. Give others the same freedom to be themselves that you yourself need. *Don't try to impose your will on another's.* Keep things from turning into power struggles.

Conflict is a natural part of most jobs. To do what you do well will cause you to bump heads with those whose performance is based on differing strengths. The key is to keep doing what you do well—with their help. Joint purposes lead to appreciation of otherwise undervalued actions.

**Tension:** "Do as I say, not as I do" was one of my father's favorite ways to tease me into recognizing he was not always right. But he expected me to understand that "the system" did have expectations of how things were to be done. There was a certain tension in knowing I couldn't get away with the Quick Start talents he used because a girl wasn't expected to become an entrepreneur (not back in the '50s). I surely would be better off if I learned to conform to expectations, if I got a graduate degree and letters after my name. Maybe then I'd have the authority to be outspoken.

No, I'd have to to do things my own way, I determined, as I turned down admission to graduate studies. It was as if a weight had been lifted off my shoulders. The tension I'd been under dissipated immediately. In choosing to march to my own drummer, I'd moved with my conative instincts.

Those who deny their potential in order to fulfill the expectations of others suffer a tension not only internally, but externally, with the source of those expectations. Resistant Fact Finders usually have a special disgust for the educational system that forced them into such a mode of operation. An Implementor who never got encouragement to follow his instincts might sense tension with the parent who disdained his talents. Resistant Follow Thrus in an organization often cause intentional problems for those responsible for their adhering to procedures. The

tension between a resistant Quick Start and one who demands an immediate response is often visible. People dig
their heels in to keep from being pushed into roles for
which they are unsuited.

*Tension* is the most easily remedied of the conative
causes of stress. All that is necessary is for others to expect
of you what you know is do-able. However, not many
people are open about their resistance, so the I-can-do-
whatever-it-takes syndrome reinforces the tension of false
expectations from others.

You may know perfectly well you won't take a physical
risk, but you talk a good game. Your friends expect you to
jump off the cliff into the water. That's tension.

You know it's not your thing to go into the family business, but the folks are sure you're well suited to the role.
That's tension.

Tension is an unnecessary by-product of lack of conative
knowledge. The workplace is rife with trainers, management consultants, and managers who think they know
how everyone should perform, yet don't know anything
of the instincts behind productivity. No amount of training, cajoling, or force can make one person live up to the
expectations of another, and only letting go of unrealistic
demands can remove the source of conative tension. The
greatest initial benefit of introducing the conative concept
into an organization is the dissipation of tension.

## Personal Performance

Our sense of achievement on the job diminishes in direct proportion to the discrepancy between our Job-KCI
and personal KCI results. In fact, this discrepancy is the

root cause of what are all too often labeled personality conflicts or inability to withstand pressure. By comparing job requirements and expectations as reflected in the Job-KCI with instinctive capabilities as seen in the KCI, it is possible to measure the degree of job-related stress. A discrepancy of 4 units in any one mode between the two indexes causes intolerable stress and inhibits individual performance. At 5 percent per unit, that's 20 percent of your mental energy that's working at cross purposes.

### Inhibitors of Personal Performance

| TYPE OF STRESS | 20-PERCENT DISPARITY BETWEEN |
| --- | --- |
| Strain | personal KCI and own Job-KCI |
| Conflict | KCI results of two individuals working interdependently |
| Tension | personal KCI and others' Job-KCI performance requirements and needs |

All three forms of conative stress inhibit personal performance because they interfere with the use of innate capabilities. Instead of all mental energy being directed toward goals, achievement is side-tracked as effort has to be made to confront the sources of stress. If you first have to convince yourself you can do the job, or others that you can do it your own way, that commitment of your greatest natural resource limits the effort available to achieve presumably greater goals. If all you can say at the end of the day is "At least I got a chance to try it my own way," it's a necessary step, but it's just a beginning.

Since organizations are essentially hiring mental energy when they put a person on the payroll, and therefore expect a commitment of it, the loss of effort through conative strain, conflict, or tension can be assessed in dollar terms. A $40,000-a-year supervisor with 25-percent stress is only working at three-quarters capacity. That adds up to a $10,000 annual loss from his personal performance. When 20 of 100 managers are suffering equal loss through stress, the bottom line cost is $200,000 and a 20-percent depletion of overall effort.

Organizations that recognize that all achievements come through individuals working interactively learn to provide opportunities for success. Such opportunities are always based on making the "how" of jobs fit the individual instead of individuals having to conform to pre-established expectations.

It is not only your prerogative to be true to your own instincts, it is imperative for you to act according to your own will. The same being true for every person in your world, there are obvious advantages to reinforcing the strengths of those around you, utilizing differences, and avoiding resistances. This simple concept, when acted upon within organizations, has more than doubled productivity.

A life insurance general agent had won awards for performance, but until he acted on the KCI results of all those in his agency, it had not begun to reach its potential. He brought a Fact Finder/Follow Thru in from field sales and put him in charge of administration, and released Quick Start energy in a couple of others who were being held back by operational responsibilities. In his own case, he freed himself to use his 9 in Quick Start to bring in business and quit trying to act like a manager. Strain, conflict, and tension were minimized, so that people who later admitted they were on the verge of quitting became star performers. The agency won an unprecedented award for greatest increase in productivity three years in a row.

Remember that whatever the role, you have to do it your way to do it successfully. Your conative character cannot be changed to suit a particular situation. With a little guidance, you can learn to direct your efforts through specific modes as needed, but you can't call on strengths you don't have.

# – 4 –

# Creating Synergy

It might have been in a movie house a long time ago or last week on Saturday afternoon TV, but we've all seen Judy Garland and Mickey Rooney singing their hearts out in somebody's barn or backyard. It seems Mickey was always the Quick Start who uttered that famous phrase: "Hey, kids—let's-put-on-a-show!" Then it was Judy, the Follow Thru, who said, "Okay. Let's see, we'll need someone to make the costumes," and, "Leave it to me. I'll arrange for everything." There were always plenty of tap dancers and set builders around with Implementor skills. Perhaps the Fact Finder was offstage, because there was no apparent management of the situation. People broke into song without the slightest provocation.

I've seen a lot of companies use that same kind of spontaneous organizational development. They put their act together by targeting their energies on the specific performance. Everyone in the cast supports the effort and they pull it off. I've also worked with quite different outfits that spend months—even years—designing elaborate strategic plans. What I've found is that, no matter how good the plan is or how apt the planners, if all the players don't buy in, the show doesn't come off.

I especially enjoy consulting with companies that have a strong mission statement. A sense of mission is a prerequisite for targeting individual talents toward synergistic efforts.

Lofty statements such as "Improve conditions for mankind" do not make for measurable conative goals, but stay in the affective or emotional domain. While we may readily agree on the desire, it doesn't help direct activity. I can only wish such organizations well.

The Kolbe Concept can help when the goal is to build more housing, discover cures, organize protection, design systems, seek economic alternatives. With such a sense of organizational purpose, there is a basis for allocating people power, a place to focus it, a compelling challenge, and tangibles to demonstrate.

Organizational development issues are fundamentally conative concerns because they start with collective commitment, whether the organization is a sports team, a business, or a charitable group. The force behind collective MOs can then be directed, and the show can go into the performance stage. Without commitment to common goals, mental energies can end up targeted unproductively, or even counterproductively.

Once organizational goals are clearly in mind, the next step is to quantify the conative talent on board. If you have all singers, you may have to drop the dance numbers. If you have a bunch of Fact Finder/Follow Thru performers, don't expect to develop and promote new technology. If innovation is your goal, you'll need an influx of Quick Start. Maybe it's there. You just haven't looked deep enough into the organization, and part of the reason is that until now you haven't been able to identify just what it was you were looking for.

## The Four Obstacles to Organizational Effectiveness

No organization can succeed unless the individuals within it have the freedom to be themselves. The multiplier effect of uninhibited personal performances is the formula for reaching group goals.

When groups fail to reach objectives, the causes can include lack of cognitive skills or knowledge, or lack of sufficient motivation (either cognitive or affective). But, when otherwise qualified members of the team have made committed effort and the results are not satisfactory, the problems are conative.

At the most basic level, there are four major organizational problems that the Kolbe Concept pinpoints:

Inertia
Polarization
Depletion
Meltdown

### Inertia

Uniformity of talent—which is another way of saying the lack of conative diversity—limits opportunity. *Inertia* abounds in organizations that select conative clones—people with very similar KCI results. Such people reinforce one another to the point that they are sure everything is just fine—even while they have no competitive advantage and are missing opportunities for growth. It's tough to tell a group of highly qualified people working on a project that the very fact they are all so compatible may be a problem. I might even urge them to bring back the guy who insisted on more detailed planning.

When you're busy, it's tempting to want to multiply yourself, to have more than one of you to get everything done. If you had someone with the same knack, you wouldn't have to tell them how to do things; they'd just naturally do them your way. Maybe it would be a duplication of talent, but that might be exactly what you think you need.

Sometimes it is. It's been a solution for many salespeople who needed to divide their territories among independent producers, landscapers who had an overload of work to pass on, teachers who needed substitutes, park rangers working in tandem to put out fires, secretaries on split shifts.

But some pairs, like bookends, need opposite strengths. In rodeo contests, the Implementor bull riders need the Quick Start clown scurrying underfoot to save them from disaster. But in pairs where people are totally reliant on each other, going for complete opposites is not necessarily the solution either. The clown has to have enough Implementor to have a feel for what the cowboy is doing. Among ice-skating pairs, conative conflicts could cause hooked skates. Often, I've observed that the female in that situation has strong insistences and resistances which set the tone for the performance, and the male is a Facilitator who can accommodate either her flair or her technical expertise. He holds her while she does the death spiral.

Members of teams with individual contributors, such as gymnastics, can differ widely in MOs, yet on a soccer team complementary differences are the key to winning. A team of all Quick Starts would run chaotically around, resisting the coach's plan of action, a field full of loose cannons. All Fact Finders, strategizing every play and arguing every official's call would turn it into more of a chess match.

Yet, even when we need it least, there's a natural tendency to try to get people to conform to our way of doing things. After all, if it works best for us, why wouldn't we expect that's the way others should work?

We all get comfortable with our own way of doing things, so, whether or not it would add synergy to the equation, we'd just as soon not open the doors to another way. If you have worked for three people in a row who do things the same way, you'll hope for a similar person next time. If you're a Quick Start, you may prefer to keep brainstorming rather than be pinned down by others who insist on accountability. Perhaps it's less mentally invigorating, but it's easier.

What happens with a room full of insistent Fact Finders? Nothing. They sit around and discuss things, but never have quite enough data to make a decision.

What happens with a room full of resistant Fact Finders? Nothing. Nobody is setting priorities or being practical.

What happens in a room full of Follow Thrus? Nothing.

Without input from others there's nothing to coordinate.

What about a room with all resistant Follow Thrus? Nothing. There's no focus.

What happens when the room is full of Quick Start insistence? Chaos.

Quick Start resistance? No risk-taking. Nothing new and different.

What about a room of insistent Implementors? It's empty. They've gone outside.

Implementor resistance? Those folks are on the phone trying to reach repair people.

There may be fewer confrontations among conative clones, but it's not the stuff of synergy.

If you are in an organization made up of conative clones, you probably find it boring. The same problems come up over and over and never seem to find solutions. One company I work with had a division in which more than 70 percent of the people were insistent in Fact Finder or Follow Thru and more than half were resistant in Quick Start.

|      | INSISTENT (%) | ACCOMMODATING (%) | RESISTANT (%) |
| ---- | ------------- | ----------------- | ------------- |
| FF   | 76            | 24                | 0             |
| FT   | 72            | 21                | 7             |
| QS   | 11            | 31                | 58            |
| I    | 12            | 48                | 40            |

The division operated independently, with its own sales and marketing functions as well as product development and manufacturing. Frankly, unless it had been a pure research group or had some other appropriately separate function, it didn't matter what the product or service was, it wasn't going to be a healthy organization. That it was a free-standing business group meant it would topple of its own top-heavy Fact Finder/Follow Thru weight.

It did. Within a year the company had tossed in the towel on the division and dispersed the people from it into several other divisions.

I've found inertia in an emergency services firm that required adherence to Follow Thru procedures to such an overwhelming degree that everyone promoted from within came with that strength. Over a 20-year period, the entire management team and all levels beneath it became populated with insistent Follow Thru. But, because the strength was also consistently accompanied by resistance in Quick Start, no new systems came into being and new equipment hadn't been purchased. Instead of responding to the changing needs of the community, this organization was responding to its own internal rituals.

Another outfit with no forward momentum was chock-full of Quick Start. Anyone with less than 6 in this mode would quit in frustration because of unmitigated chaos, or would be fired for the inability to keep several projects going at once. The sense of urgency kept everyone in motion—but it merely kept them darting without hitting any targets.

Some organizations are going a hundred miles an hour and welcome the inertia of not trying to pick up more steam. Others are made up of independent producers who band together to cover overheads. Professional teams of doctors, lawyers, or accountants rarely exude synergistic differences. But, then, they rarely do more together than divvy up the bounty.

When individuals do need to function as a team, conative cloning is the surest path to lost opportunities. Instead of offsetting one another's resistances, they limit their range of capabilities. Instead of managing natural conflicts and being stimulated by differing perspectives, conative look-alikes smugly reinforce their singlemindedness.

Am I against things being easy? Yes. Mental complacency may be comfortable, but it is not productive. It keeps individuals from fulfilling their destiny and organizations from their goals. We all seek to find the path of least resistance, but some degree of conflict is essential; team efforts require combining individual talents into synergy. That means working with people who bring different strengths to the table.

## Polarization

The Fact Finders clone themselves in one area of the organization and the Quick Starts stick together in another, compounding the problem with *polarization.*

Polarization is seen most dramatically in labor/management disputes, in which there may be a mix of Fact Finder and Quick Start dominances on one side of the table, talking to Implementor insistent craftsmen and Follow Thru service people on the other. Each Action Mode responds differently to external stimuli, which is why there is a need for a variety of incentives.

While management is giving facts and figures and trying to get workers to respond favorably to change, the labor force is pulling in the opposite direction. The workers want Implementor quality assurance and Follow Thru guarantees of continuity. Management's fact sheets and the workers' demands are at odds because neither side responds constructively to the other's approach. They're working at cross purposes.

Within the organization, polarization between departments is a frequent cause of friction. The Follow Thru service group is accused of not being responsive to the Quick Starts in sales. The Fact Finder strategists never make a decision within the time frame promised the Follow Thrus, who have to monitor cash-flow projections. Implementors in the field have too much paperwork because of the needs of their Fact Finder supervisors. Mental energy going toward internal combat is stolen from productive purposes.

Organizations meeting productivity goals show an uncanny similarity in their distribution of mental energy. Every such company we have studied has approximately 25 percent of its combined mental energy in the insistent zone, another 25 percent in the resistant zone, and 50 percent of all effort going toward accommodation.

| | INSISTENT (%) | ACCOMMODATING (%) | RESISTANT (%) |
|---|---|---|---|
| FF | 35 | 52 | 13 |
| FT | 20 | 38 | 42 |
| QS | 40 | 42 | 18 |
| I | 5 | 68 | 27 |

Percentage of total mental energy (average)

| 25% | 50% | 25% |
|---|---|---|

When this natural balance is lost to a higher degree of insistence and resistance, often caused by over-specialization, the organization suffers losses in productivity. With so much potentially productive energy devoted to finding a compromise, polarization acts as a brake on the forward momentum that results from synergy.

A customer suffers from the polarization in a company when its Quick Start people generate ads that depict immediacy of response yet its service department employees offer slow but dependable Follow Thru service. A college that attracts students because of its well-publicized alternative educational philosophy may polarize Fact Finder faculty and Implementor/Quick Start students.

Communities become polarized on political issues with conative overtones. Implementor naturalists protest physically when the environment isn't preserved, and Fact Finder corporate analysts seek to explain economic priorities. Follow Thru teachers holding onto tenure are polarized against Quick Start/Fact Finder school board members who argue for merit-based pay. Implementor tradespeople fighting to protect handcrafted quality are polarized against Follow Thrus who would mass-produce.

## Depletion

In most cases where I find a company in trouble, by comparing KCIs with Job-KCIs we can demonstrate that a high percentage of its key people are resistant in the very mode necessary for it to reach its goals—they are suffering from strain. This *depletion* of mental resources within an organization comes when a high percentage of those within it try to perform in ways unnatural to them.

Mental energy works against itself when you deny your conative instincts. If you're working in a group, your loss is reflected in its bottom line. Productivity in an organization decreases by the sum of all the effort lost through such strain.

Sometimes organizational issues increase the probability of depletion. Believing in their own press coverage has caused sports teams, acting companies, and auto manufacturers to change tactics and perform "as advertised." A bunch of resistant Implementors in basketball began playing a more physical game and lost in the national playoffs. An old-line Gilbert and Sullivan theatrical company that thought it would try nontraditional shows lost its regular audiences—and received some bad reviews. A car manufacturing company known for quality construction and boring body design introduced a sleeker model that didn't conform to its usual standards. It, too, lost its niche. In every case, the pain was self-inflicted, and the resulting strain on the people involved led to depletion of the group's productivity.

Using the conative connection to help employees decrease strain and the other forms of stress is always beneficial for the company as well. When a person is out of sync with himself, it always saps strength from group effort. Depletion is self-imposed but hurts others. As with any artificial means of functioning, it causes those around the person to suffer. It limits the ability to predict how a person will act, react, and interact.

Because modern Western culture rarely rewards Implementor insistence as highly as the other modes—except in athletics—many an artisan seeks promotion to more highly paid office jobs. The finest tool-and-die maker becomes plant manager, the most proficient chemist is out seeking research grants. In organizations dependent upon hands-on talent, the very way it's rewarded can cause depletion.

A good surgeon is rarely the best choice for hospital planning committees. Usually, there's been the good sense not to select hospital administrators from the medical pool. Yet depleting the ranks to fill first-line supervisor jobs in manufacturing, to turn investigative reporters into editors, to select principals from schoolteachers, is common practice. What has been called "Peter-Principling" is often a matter of having taken a person out of his conative strengths.

Depletion costs organizations more than it would take to reward people for the committed use of their talents. Companies I help decrease depletion benefit from lowering levels of absenteeism, work-related accidents, and incidents of substance abuse and gain significantly higher ratings on employee satisfaction. Funds spent on treating symptoms of stress can be earmarked for conatively sensitive incentive programs.

## Meltdown

Meltdown occurs when people who know perfectly well who they are suffer from unrealistic, external, rather than self-imposed, pressure to act otherwise. Meltdown exists when managers' Job-KCIs differ widely from employee's KCIs. Or when changes in an industry or the economy require different MOs than those on hand. Or when closely held companies are passed down to a generation that hasn't the necessary conative capabilities of the founders. Or when mergers and takeovers lead to a mish-mash of management in which protecting fiefdoms is a higher priority than maximizing productivity.

Meltdown of mental energy takes place because there isn't recognition of the conative connection. People with a "sales personality" are given jobs that require cold calling and closing deals, which means Quick Start risk-taking. I have found no correlation between action orientation and results on personality inventories. The extrovert in the crowd may be the last one who would ask for the sale. My research shows most successful salespeople have at least a 6 in Quick Start, but that there is no correlation with personality type or preferences.

I suspect a Facilitator would have the best MO for a school principal. But you have to be a teacher first, which is a role more suited to Follow Thrus and Fact Finders. What happens when you have to go through chairs that don't fit you comfortably in order to get to your proper place at the table? The Quick Start who would have made a marvelous trial attorney quits law school. The colorist gets discouraged in drawing classes and drops art. The innovator who could have brought new technology to the firm gets tired of being told to conform and goes elsewhere.

As long as you can see light at the end of the tunnel, you can survive conative restrictions. If the light is too distant or shows no promise of being there at all, you are best to seek other options.

Investment banking firms have a reputation for chewing up and spitting out the brightest young talent around in two-year stints as project analysts. The extremely high salaries are attractive at first, but people conatively capable of long-term success in the industry soon drop out. While the hours are long, that's not what they complain about. One woman told me she left for half the pay and just as much work, "but I won't be treated inhumanly—as if I go on automatic pilot and don't have a mind for more than detailed data." Companies lose out on needed talent when they treat people as robots—"things" with no conative instinct.

Many an assembly-line operation dehumanizes in much the same way. If you expect peak performance from people, you have to provide opportunities to be more than one-dimensional. If employees are required to work within a Follow Thru system, provide them with breaks for recreational Implementor activities—outdoor sports if possible, or a craft center. Provide Fact Finder outlets, such as a library, or word puzzles and strategic games. Challenge their Quick Start with contests and let them know there is a time and place where they can offer original ideas.

## Avoiding Obstacles

| CAUSE | EFFECT | PRESCRIPTION |
| --- | --- | --- |
| Cloning | Inertia | Change selection process; use outside resources. |
| Conflict | Polarization | Mediate roles; barter talents. |
| Strain | Depletion | Clarify goals; review options. |
| Tension | Meltdown | Redefine rules; restructure tasks. |

Burnout is greatest in firms that don't provide options for how people perform. I've found that many professional partnerships ignore the conative needs of mid-level people, insisting they conform to set patterns of performance. After about three years, strong-minded people who don't fit the mold go on their way.

Most employee retention problems are conative. People will buy their way out of situations that lock them into lack of personal fulfillment. A coach whose athletic director or owner is imposing his own no-risk style may buy out his contract and go somewhere that allows him the freedom to use his Quick Start intuition. A professional who is pigeonholed in a Follow Thru slot may move on to opportunities with a broader range of options. A technician who has been an independent contributor may seek alternative employment when he's forced out of an Implementor role into a Fact Finder manager position.

Unfortunately, most outplacement programs emphasize work experience without the knowledge that success is tied to instinct. But with the proper counseling, people who have felt unfulfilled on the job need not go back into the same lion's den.

An office manager with the ideal MO for a sales position went on more than twenty interviews before someone gave her a chance to prove her mettle. She was the top in her sales group by the end of the first six months. A man with the natural instinct of a graphic designer, a strong Follow Thru, only discovered his ultimate career path by having to fill in for the regular designer on staff. When he'd gone for career counseling he was told his personality characteristics suited him for sales, but he knew deep down that that wasn't his forte.

The type of resume writing that goes on today is pretty useless both to the employer and the applicant. People address the way they would *like* to perform, how they think employers would *want* them to function, but don't have the information at hand to explain what they actually *will* contribute. The resume is useless when it is a catch-all. A summary of where a person has worked offers few clues as to what they do best. It only recapitulates history without predicting the future.

A defense contractor had a division loaded with Fact Finder and Quick Start dominance—the great justifiers and the great improvisors. Their KCI results demonstrated not only that, as an organization, they were dealing from a very limited deck, but that they were also missing the trump card. Nobody in a position of responsibility was strong in Follow Thru, the patterning mode of the regulator who would insist on compliance. Everyone on the management team had, in fact, a score of 3 or below in Follow Thru, meaning that each and every one of them was constitutionally *resistant* to following procedures.

As I pointed to all the bar graphs with the very short blue lines for Follow Thru, I cautioned that staying within rigid budgetary guidelines and maintaining systems and procedures would be a problem for this group. I then told them they could expect trouble if they didn't bring some Follow Thru insistence into the equation. It wasn't that the others *couldn't* carry out these functions, it was just that no one *would*. It was not in anyone's nature to *insist,* to be by nature profoundly adverse to the absence of policy adhered to and procedures carried out.

Unfortunately, this firm had come to me too late, and within a few weeks the news hit the papers that they had been slapped with a multi-million-dollar fine for noncompliance with government regulations. Heads rolled, simply because these smart, energetic, and otherwise competent people had been unprotected by conative checks and balances. It is this same conative deficit in Follow Thru, combined with a lack of Implementor, that causes innumerable industrial accidents. One client found that every employee involved in a work-related accident over the previous two years had 4 units or less of Follow Thru. Even though they had attended regular training programs, they had neglected to follow standard safety procedures.

Conative resistance is always a stress point for the individual, but that also makes it a source of many of the problems managers have to face every day. For each Action Mode, those problems are different.

**Fact Finder Resistance**
ignores past experience
acts inappropriately
doesn't deal with complexities
pays no attention to detail
is not strategically oriented

**Follow Thru Resistance**
avoids procedures
fights the system
uses time inefficiently
is noncompliant
lacks completion

**Quick Start Resistance**
lacks a sense of urgency
resists change

has difficulty dealing with ambiguity
is inflexible
won't take risks

**Implementor Resistance**
ignores durability factors
doesn't deal well with tangibles
lacks sensitivity to product quality
doesn't maintain plant and equipment
puts off making repairs

One government-regulated company in a foreign country had been told publicly that it either had to stop resisting needed changes or its charter would be lifted. When we went in and analyzed the problem, we found that 83 percent of its managers were resistant in Quick Start and none insistent in it. We had to show them how to deal with change by doing it in increments, complete with detailed explanations of what was staying the same, in order to satisfy the needs of their Fact Finder/Follow Thru work force. Demands that employees make changes, take risks, and innovate had only added to their stress. Training managers in how to bring about desired results by building on the strengths available was the most practical solution.

The internal stress of a group's working against its own instincts is so great that eventually it will collapse in on itself. Effort ceases to be constructive, as meltdown leads to bankruptcies, unfriendly takeovers, and other forms of failure.

When deregulation opened windows of opportunity, savings and loan institutions with Fact Finder and Follow Thru talent on board tried to become growth-oriented

Quick Start outfits. What resulted was the meltdown of an entire industry. In the same way, many a Quick Start venture fails when it doesn't bring in sufficient Fact Finder and Follow Thru to manage growth.

The way to rid an organization of inertia is to bring in differing MOs through hiring; promotion; the use of advisors, consultants, and board members; or calling on professional associations.

Polarization can be decreased by separation of responsibilities that keep such groups from having to function interactively. Since it would take a quantity of differing insistences to significantly alter the extremes, a lesser injection of Facilitators would dramatically alter the mix and create a more synergistic team.

Removing the obstacles caused by depletion and meltdown requires fine-tuning both expectations and positioning of talents. Often, shuffling people into more suitable slots on organizational charts allows for more productive use of capabilities. Managers can be trained to build on workers' strengths rather than trying to force unncessary conative conformity.

Depletion, of all the obstacles, is the one which responds best to seminar-format solutions. I find most managers willing to offer opportunities for success when they realize the roadblocks that have inhibited performance. And most employees value the chance to prove themselves, once they realize the deck won't be stacked against them.

When meltdown is pervasive in an organization, removing it takes committed effort. Since it's precisely that element that's been missing, the process we put a company through becomes the catalyst for a solution.

## Team-Building

Talking about conative problems doesn't make them go away. They have to be identified, quantified, and then resolved through action. At one time, the biggest problem for the Chicago Bulls was having one of basketball's greatest players on their team. Singlehandedly scoring record numbers of points—often half the team's total—Michael Jordan cost the Bulls many games by his overwhelming dominance of their offense. He'd shoot from any place on the floor. He'd take any opponent on one-on-one. He was the team.

Here was a Quick Start (I presume) who could do it all, but Jordan wasn't the cause of the problem. An unselfish player, he asked management for a supporting cast, and when at last they teamed him with other shooters like Craig Hodges who played an altogether different kind of game, the Bulls started winning more consistently. They were no longer a one-dimensional team. The synergy of a Follow Thru/Fact Finder approach brought cooperation in setting patterns and taking strategic shots. It gave Jordan the ability to dish the ball off to others who helped open up the game for the Bulls.

Some businesses use the term "individual contributor" for those whose talents are valued, but who aren't necessarily expected to mesh into the framework of the organization. They're the stars who aren't required to play ball with the rest.

The most innovative engineer in one firm was so different from the conative norm in the company that he was pulled out of his work group, given an office cut off from the others, and asked to design products that would assure the company's future. His role was so key that he wasn't asked to sit in on any policy meetings or to participate in day-to-day functions. But what he came up with in his isolation disturbed senior management.

"What's wrong with Henry? Has he gone off the deep end? There's no way we can use what he's giving us," they said. "Kathy, tell us why he's not producing."

To know whether the problem was even in my field of expertise, I first needed to see how he was performing. Maybe it would have nothing to do with conation. Perhaps he was feeling pressured, or the praise had gone to his head—both affective problems.

What I discovered was that he was performing beautifully, only not for the team that was paying him. His efforts to originate products were being made in cooperation with clients. When the company cut him off from mental interactions he'd lost the synergistic benefit of having others critique his work, suggest alternatives, and question assumptions. All he had to go on was 20 units of mental energy, not the multiple of that which comes from joint efforts. As is usually true of strongly insistent people, he needed others to fill in the gaps in his MO, and he turned to end-users of the systems he was designing. They were happy to work with him on new concepts which they hoped his company would produce for them.

In essence the company had been providing some of its customers with unbilled consulting. The engineer's brainpower was addressing external problems, not internal corporate goals. His efforts produced plans that fascinated the customers and were totally out of line for the company that was paying for them.

When a company puts a person on the payroll, it generally assumes it's adding to its own productivity. It expects performance, yet, if a person is brought in as an "individual contributor," the amount of mental energy being hired can never exceed 20 units. When a person is brought in as a team member, the result can be magnified by synergy.

When the Bulls brought in skilled players who complemented Jordan's MO, they not only had others contributing to the play, but Jordan's own efforts also improved.

This conative connection is one reason independent salespeople and stand-alone professionals join associations. Minds meet at conventions and workshops, stimulating each other's activity and filling in the conative voids. Resistant Fact Finders can hear industry summaries. The resistant Quick Start can find boiler-plate promo pieces or at least get some ideas for how to do them. Resistant Implementors might purchase prefabricated display panels. Resistant Follow Thrus will usually seek out the prepackaged software or business formulas.

Having people in the next room doesn't assure synergy. It's surprising how many management teams are not teams at all. Loneliness—lack of synergy—doesn't just happen at the top. Having no one to spark off of is a major problem at all levels.

The general manager of a Fortune 500 division told me he'd never had to work in such a void as when he made it to the top. He'd cut himself off from the synergistic effect because of an affective fear of looking as if he didn't know what he was doing. He mistakenly felt that being in charge meant having to solve problems on his own. If he needed someone else, he felt as if he wasn't needed.

A heavily unionized company asked me to analyze problems with its first-line supervisors. I found they were caught between the workers, who thought of them as the enemy, and their own superiors, who didn't consider them a part of management. The walls built between work groups didn't allow them horizontal or peer support either. Their isolation was so obvious that those under them said that they would reject a promotion to the position.

"Every day I go it alone," one supervisor told me. "I have no one to suggest alternatives, just people who don't like what I'm doing. I get what I think is a good idea and there's no one to bounce it off of. The first time I see the holes in it is when one of the people I supervise asks why I did this or didn't do that. I work in a company with thousands of people but I don't have anyone on my team."

Protecting one's turf is one of the major detriments to team building, as it causes workers to lock out talents that could be put to productive use. It's a symptom of either over-specialization or internal politics, and should be taken as a warning of needed organizational reforms.

## Bartering Your Natural Resources

Many partnerships are made up of people with the same talent who merely share overhead. They have a common receptionist, use the same copy machine and allocate telephone expenses. Other partnerships actually do joint casework. They go in teams to visit clients and have partnership meetings to discuss how they'll interact on an account. Between them they find solutions. Depending on the talent necessary, any one of the partners could be brought into a case.

Another version of a partnership is one where the members barter their services with each other. One person brings in a case that remains his, but, because he isn't a specialist on a particular topic, he'll turn part of the project over to a partner. Partners don't try to intrude in each other's areas of specialization and don't spend much time interacting. The difference between working as a team and bartering your conative talent for another's is that, with a team, you have to stick around and help out. When you barter, you can walk away. (If you agree to take over my research, I don't expect to be involved in any way. Tag, you're it. I'm on to something else.)

As long as all the players understand the rules to this conative game, everything is fine. Problems arise when one partner expects input from the others and doesn't get it, or thinks he's bartered his services and finds all he's doing is sharing expenses. He's just put out a conative IOU that has been torn up without his knowing it. Giving money to an economic partnership is very different from giving of yourself.

A national sales rep was given first-class plane tickets by his company, on the theory he would be more likely to sit next to decision-makers to whom he could sell during the trip. He discovered he rarely had enough Quick Start energy left to do any promoting of the product while sitting in his upgraded seats. A man of principle, he traded them in for the freedom to relax his mental energy.

Arriving home mentally exhausted causes office problems to spill over into home situations. When you walk in the door, little kids expect you to be as fresh as when you left in the morning. Even spouses who also work have no way of knowing just what you've been through that day.

Bartering with family members to lay off you the first few minutes you get home from work isn't a bad idea. Tell them you'll devote your full energy to the game they want to play—later—if they'll give you half an hour of peace and quiet. Or say you'll cook dinner every night next week if you can get out of all responsibilities the night before a major presentation.

All this works pretty well, unless the mental energy you've bargained away is all gone when you need to offer it. Catch a Quick Start when she's in her stride and she'll take on thirty-six new challenges. But don't ask one who's trying to come up with a new slogan at work to help write your ad at night. After she's got her slogan, then ask.

But if you expect someone to do something for you as a result of what you've done for them, you'll have to communicate it. Otherwise they may think you're in one of those partnerships based on sharing overhead or helping each other out on a team basis. Bartering causes problems when only one person in the transaction thinks that's what's happening.

## Overcoming Conative Deficits

Even when it's a team that's playing, it doesn't always function as a conative or functional unit. To be effective it requires someone to manage it, just as any good sports team needs a coach. And, even then, the coach needs others with whom he can interact. Coaches join associations. If they're good they're probably using assistants effectively. They may also bring in consultants and build a team of advisors who add to the equation. Any coach who doesn't do so is limited to those 20 units of brain power within his own MO. There's only so much he can do.

Members of synergistic teams have different conative strengths. They may also differ cognitively or affectively, causing intellectual debates or value-oriented schisms. When you're working with others, how do you separate how much you think alike and how much you are alike conatively? Does the assistant coach agree with the strategy because it's the smartest thing to do or because he's a fellow Fact Finder?

A good way to look at the difference is to consider a Fact Finder accountant advising a Quick Start entrepreneur on how to keep travel and entertainment records. Their *thoughts* on what needs to be done may coincide completely. But, if the accountant assumes the Quick Start (who, let's say, is also resistant to Follow Thru) will actually *do* what they agreed upon, he hasn't advised many entrepreneurs before. The Quick Start will probably stay with the plan for a short time and then sidestep it. He may just dump stuff in a drawer and construct the records if and when he gets audited. Even though that haphazard method has worked for a number of my entrepreneurial clients, only the one with a Quick Start tax accountant has ever been told it was an acceptable alternative.

Errors made in a baseball game often occur because fielders expect another player to be there. The baseball farm system makes it difficult for a team-oriented player to excel, because it promotes those who stand out. If an infielder tries to make an over-the-shoulder catch rather than letting the outfielder take it, the team might lose the out but the player has a greater chance to look good. When he gets to the majors the player will need to function synergistically. There, winning games is the goal for most players. Individual performers have to contribute to that effort.

A franchising organization asked me to help determine why some of its owners met every expectation, including running very profitable stores, and why others frequently had difficulties. Franchises are based on a consistent quality of product and service. The parent company offers the same opportunity for success to those who guarantee standardized performance in return. Every fast food burger, for instance, is supposed to be the same size and served in the same way.

Taking into account location, years in the business, and other such variables, there still was a significant discrepancy in performance. I was asked if, based on KCI results, I could help select people with the greatest probability of succeeding in running their own franchised operations.

I gave the KCI to several highly productive managers and to several of the lowest performers. There was no one MO that seemed to determine success, except having Follow Thru in at least the accommodating zone. However, when I asked each manager to do Job-KCIs for the positions on their teams and indexed the people filling those jobs, I found significant results. First of all, there was a strong correlation between high performance at the location and team members' MOs matching the managers' Job-KCI requirements. Those managers who had matched their perceived needs with employees' capabilities had smooth-running operations. When such teamwork wasn't in evidence, performance suffered.

There was great variance in managers' expectations for identically titled positions. A dominant Fact Finder manager often sought someone with more Quick Start to be his top assistant. Again, the particular MO was not as important to bottom-line results as the person's having the conative characteristics necessary to perform in the manner expected by his manager.

*A team is as good as:*
• the conative fit each player has with his individual role
• the members are in accurately predicting the differences among themselves
• the management of the team is in using the talent available

*The best teams are those which:*
• develop the innate talents of the individuals within the team
• place people in roles in which they can find personal fulfillment
• communicate expectations for individual contributors as they relate to organizational goals
• manage all effort as a creative process, in which each individual has a personal stake as well as a group responsibility
• anticipate conflict and direct it toward constructive purposes, so that it becomes synergistic.

Sports teams make excellent analogies for businesses, because there is an immediate payoff—a win—and because the synergistic effort is so apparent. The basic principles given above are clearly necessary in developing team play. Individual contributors need to be playing the right positions, but they also have to be commited to the total effort. If a person's mind isn't on the game, all the athletic ability in the world won't undo the damage.

When effort is directed toward joint purposes, individual talents will come to the fore. There won't be the time or energy to put into negatives.

## Communication—A Conative Process

A company on the move in its marketplace hired a new director of communications whose first assignment was to produce the annual report. He was also responsible for public relations and monthly newsletters. He'd been on the job eight months when his CEO asked me to figure out why this experienced person had produced so little. With a KCI of 8723, the young man had set up a system for doing everything to meet the first objective before he went on to the second. The newsletters had to come out every month, so that was the first priority he addressed. He produced thorough, accurate, and timely articles, but the interviews and refinements took up all his time. The annual report and the PR wasn't getting done. He told me there was no need for concern—the annual report would be the best they ever had.

"The best annual report," the CEO said, "is one that comes out on time and doesn't cause any uproar."

"That's just why they need me," the communications director said. "They don't pay any attention to the details, to the lasting record this provides. People make decisions to buy our stock based on this, and I want every aspect of it to be perfect. No more slightly out-of-focus pictures. No more typefaces that don't go together."

"He may be excellent at what he does," said the CEO. "If so, I don't want excellence."

The "communicator" wanted to be so "right" that he didn't get a printer's bid on the project until the exact layout was completed. No rounding off for him. That cost three weeks' time, the CEO estimated. "I want credibility. But we don't need to pore over every damn picture and headline. A few of them can stink. I want it done."

Had this CEO taken the time to structure assignments in ways her subordinate could act on them, she could have saved everyone a great deal of grief. A Quick Start boss needs freedom to be herself, but communicating is the one area in which you have to compromise your conative self.

The CEO needed to accommodate the highly insistent Fact Finder in her communications director by assigning her own priorities for him and discussing prudent approaches. She didn't have to be as specific as he would be, but she had to meet him halfway. She had to lay out a general plan for when things had to be completed, and specify the degree of accuracy required. By the same token, the director of communications had a responsibility to obtain the information he needed by asking bottom-line questions: What's most important? What happens if it's late? How much leeway is there?

Trying to avoid conflict between people with strong conative difference is impossible. No use pretending—it will come out sooner or later. Discussing the differences doesn't resolve them. It involves them. It turns a clash of wills into a meeting of minds. You are impelled to act according to your instincts, but you can't compel others to respond the same way.

Take time to give an insistent Fact Finder all the background. Even if you are a Quick Start, don't drop the whole load on a Follow Thru all at once. Put it into context for him. Help him deal with his need for integrating it with what's already happening. Don't require an Implementor to discuss everything. When you truly commit your mental energy to the process of communicating in light of the four Action Modes, you'll get much better results.

The conative connections within a team are complex. They involve the actions of individuals with innate drives, reactions to the circumstances affecting team goals, and interactions between members and leaders. When goals are communicated, stress minimized, and conflicts resolved, the resulting synergy makes for a winning team.

# – 5 –

# Playing with Intensity

$A$sk a busy person and he'll tell you there is a rejuvenating factor that comes with reaching targeted goals. It promotes a willingness to rely on instinct. Reaching goals frees us to trust and value the conative inclinations that magnify effectiveness. Reaching goals—*doing* what it takes to get the job done—is the way to self-confidence.

When the pressure was on Joan, a Fact Finder, to figure out a solution to a complex problem, she turned to a Quick Start insistent member of the decision-making team and said, "I'll examine the practical application. But I'm counting on you to do the presentation." The Quick Start responded, "Knowing you, you'll massage the data until the time to prepare is all used up. But that's okay. I can wing it."

These were people who knew what they were about. They had confidence in their capabilities and knew how to direct their own and each other's energy. They did indeed do what they said they would do.

While everyone has the same amount of mental energy, some people are standout performers. They play with more intensity because, like a targeted laser beam, their goal-directed energy cuts through density. Effort based on experience uses Fact Finder energy to put matters into perspective and to establish specific objectives. Your sense of focus comes through targeting your units of Follow Thru, which gives you the power of concentration. Quick Start energy is magnified when you go right to the bottom line, releasing the sense of vision, of abstraction. Implementor intensity is targeted on the tangible. You recharge it by literally making, building, or physically producing a result.

## Targeting Mental Energy

Achieving a goal requires making it a priority, focusing energy on it, getting to its bottom line, and making it happen in tangible terms. In other words—if it's worth doing, it'll take all you have to give. Your sense of accomplishment comes with those tasks that require the commitment of your creative power. Even those who have won huge sums in lotteries usually continue working. That's because having goals to work toward gives us our sense of purpose.

How much mental energy can you put into an effort? If you give 100 percent of your conative self to your job, you won't have any available for family, for friends, for recreational outlets. If you work all weekend on your taxes, you may not want to play bridge Sunday evening. The two activities take too much of the same kind of energy.

Assign a percentage of total mental energy that you want to commit to each aspect of your life, and you'll probably find that just the things you *want* to do add up to more than 100 percent. Add in all the things you *have* to do that still take mental energy, and the need for targeting specific goals becomes even clearer. Overcommitting your conative self is a major cause of failure.

When a person targets mental energy to achieve the unexpected, the conative effort is called overachieving. It's a term that exemplifies the confusion between cognitive abilities measured on IQ tests, and conative effort.

Underachieving, on the other hand, is usually confused with affect. A building contractor approached me after a seminar to ask for a private consultation. "I need to know why I'm no longer as ambitious as I used to be," he said. "I don't know if I've turned lazy or just what it is that's keeping me from working as hard as I used to. I go to work every day, but I'm not getting anywhere with it."

When I met with him later it became quite clear why he had been professionally nonproductive. He'd put his mind to settling a divorce, raising two kids, and moving to a new community. It was no wonder he had "just gone through the motions" on the job. Now that he had his personal life back in order, he was ready to delve into work-related striving.

Emotions contributed to his situation, to be sure. They were the motivation for his efforts; they triggered his actions. Still, by influencing how he functioned, the affects were causing effects. His conative abilities were in need of redirecting now that he was emotionally ready.

Targeting requires the integration of all three parts of the mind. You have to know your options cognitively, choose them affectively, and deal with them conatively. Mental energy is often used independently of our conscious decisions. The notion of controlling your own destiny is nice, but it isn't possible if you can't identify and direct your own inclinations.

Some fritter away their talents, not directing them at anything purposeful, and then wonder why others seem to have more energy than they. I know a Fact Finder who got so caught up in one-upsmanship with a friend over war games that all his talent seemed to go in that directon. He woke up mentally exhausted on many mornings, to the point that he went for psychological counseling. I suggested to him that the incredible lengths he was going to in order to study his next strategic moves in the simulations were mentally draining. He found he didn't have to give up the games completely to avoid the conflict with his professional life; he simply had to keep them in perspective. Another client, a regional manager in sales, was an ace bridge player, a life master. But now she has a pressured work life and is raising two children alone. She has had the good sense to swear off bridge, having found it sapped her 5573 of mental energy.

When one of my clients complained of what was clearly conative overload, she described it in terms of physical fatigue, but the reality was that she was sleeping as many hours as she ever had. She was working in a corporate culture (lots of Fact Finder output), dealing with a sick husband, caring for her children's needs at night, and trying to maintain a schedule of community involvement. Most of what she did was from a sitting position, and she was gaining weight. Physical energy wasn't being burned, but she was going through conative energy at an unrealistic rate. She was so busy trying to do everything that she wasn't setting priorities or focusing. "Don't sweat the small stuff" is a conative directive for everyone from a Quick Start to a Fact Finder. "God is in the details" works the other way. It depends on who you are. If your energy has been consumed without result, staying in the same conative rut to try again can be debilitating. A Quick Start who is resistant in Follow Thru will get nowhere by practicing his tennis serve over and over. Working longer hours without readjusting how you are approaching a task is the worst possible solution. Mental energy continues to plummet without reward, and you are denied the leisure necessary for regeneration.

## Degrees of Effort

Playing with intensity requires targeting your efforts. How do you do this?

1. Decide where you *intend* to direct your efforts.
2. Determine the intensity you will *try* to put into those efforts.
3. *Commit* to allocating, focusing, challenging, and demonstrating your mental energy toward those efforts, as well as to conserving it for those purposes.

The key words are *intend, try* and *commit*. These are the degrees of conation. You've just begun to target your mental energy when you identify your intentions. As soon as you try, you've engaged the conative engine the next step. You're fully in gear when your actions are based on com-

mitment of your mental energy. Without commitment—
commitment to perform, to target talents on a goal—no
amount of intelligence or caring will make a person
productive.

I don't believe anyone is naturally lazy. Nor do I think
the expression "work ethic" is apt. Everyone strives; some
people just might not be targeting their efforts toward economic goals. They may be putting a great deal of effort
into not getting a particular job done. While we can't
change others conatively or determine our employees'—
or children's—MOs, we can help them to make determined use of their minds and be productive human
beings. The reason corporations need mission statements
is to hone in on what needs to be done. Helping others
target their talents is the key to quality in management—
just as it is in parenting, teaching, or any situation in
which we can help others learn to make a commitment of
their natural talents.

Targeting effort requires:
• intellectual understanding and emotional caring, to
*motivate* action
• a persistent level of intensity
• calling on the particular powers of instinctive will to
allocate Fact Finder energy, focus Follow Thru energy,
challenge Quick Start energy, and demonstrate Implementor energy
• withholding expenditure of energy in each Action
Mode to preserve it for targeted use
• releasing creative power purposefully

As Erich Fromm wrote in *Human Ethics*: "There is no
meaning to life except the meaning man gives his life by

unfolding his powers by living productively; and only constant vigilance, activity and effort can keep him from failure in the one task that matters—the full development of his powers. . . . He can make use of his powers only if he knows what they are, how to use them and what to use them for. . . ."

If you are trying to target another person's efforts, you can tap into specific strengths.

**For Fact Finder Talents:** Provide sufficient information for insistent Fact Finders to understand the specifics of an assignment. Clarify priorities and outline objectives, allowing them to restate problems or opportunities. Provide appropriate perquisites and reasonable compensation. Allow them to identify time frames and justify conditions. The best way to present a task to a Fact Finder dominant person is by saying, "These objectives need to be met because . . ."

**For Follow Thru Talents:** Provide an overview of the problem for people strong in Follow Thru, to assure dependable solutions. Have all the pieces of the puzzle available before you ask them to put it together. Assure them that there will be consistency and conformity. Praise them for efficiency and completeness, and offer understanding when interruptions are necessary. Provide an orderly work space in which they can arrange their own possessions. Follow Thrus will respond when given training or materials that enhance their systematizing efforts.

**For Quick Start Talents:** Challenge strong-willed Quick Starts by suggesting that what needs to be done may be impossible. Deadline situations are best; give them short-term projects. Quick Starts thrive in a competitive atmosphere, where compensation is based on bonuses and commissions. They want to win big and won't be content with salary alone. Let Quick Starts work intensely without watching the clock, but if they've immersed themselves in a project for several days, let them out of regular hours or assignments in return. Quick Starts pride themselves on doing the undoable, so motivate them with clearly recognized challenges.

**For Implementor Talents:** Implementors will be most productive when they can present an end product of which they can personally attest to the quality. They need tools to help them craft. An Implementor dominant person is more disgruntled over slipshod equipment than over pay scales. It is best to communicate with an Implementor through touch or with tangible examples, not in print or with a lot of words. Praise them for their strength and endurance, but don't overdo it, because they do not have a high regard for "mere words." Their sense of accomplishment comes when others pick up what they have done and see the solid product of their efforts. Implementors are particularly driven to get out of the office. They will often work very hard to achieve longer weekends or early retirement.

If you don't put an assignment into context for a Follow Thru, it won't be done as well. If a Quick Start insistent person senses no urgency to a project, it won't get his conative attention. In other words, if you ignore conative needs, don't blame others if they don't seem to be trying to accomplish what you wished them to.

Above all, the one thing that works best with any MO is having a sense of humor about what a person will and won't get done.

## Recreational Outlets

When the day is done, when you have succeeded to the extent possible in your efforts to intend, try, and commit, you may well still have energy to burn. That's what recreation—re-creation—is all about; an understanding of conation tells us that recreation is an activity that engages unused conative energy.

I have a friend who is a very strong Fact Finder. She writes and edits and reviews books. For years, one of her favorite Sunday recreations was crawling off to a quiet place with a crossword puzzle and an acrostic, both Fact Finder activities. Recently, she spent almost a year writing vocabulary books for secondary school students. Seven or eight weeks into that work she realized that doing word puzzles was no longer recreational. When one of her children remarked, in that endearing way adolescents have, "Boy, are you in a lousy mood," she put away the puzzles. It was time to switch into some Quick Start activities, her usual fall-back mode, which had been uncharacteristically contained.

To comprehend the effect of unused conative force, consider the physical energy that is often mounting in a child at the end of a long car trip. Any parent knows that it's a very good idea to let the child run it off. For adults as well, recreation involves "running it off." Mental energy needs release.

By using your conative power, you allow it to be replenished. The mind can increase its effectiveness by refilling its capacity. But it's as if you must use its full force before it can be re-energized. Recreational energy can be used to strive toward tagging a player out at second, or building a quality deck on the cabin, or playing a concerto. It can also be used to do what other people call work. People who stay after hours to figure out just one more problem, design one more program, or take another call may be riding the crest of a conative victory. They are not necessarily workaholics or Type As who do it out of affective need. Their conative drive may be in gear, and they are reenergized by their achievement.

A director of marketing at a major publishing house is a 4386 Quick Start/Implementor. He scarcely ever sits still in the office, and he generates ideas as fast as he can. A fine athlete, he needs to play, and he is a tough competitor. A typical good day for him begins early in the morning at the office and starts again as the office closes down—he's off to play a tennis match or compete in a local baseball game. When that's over, he's back in the office for a good couple of hours of work, still riding that crest and highly productive.

A recreational game of tennis, one in which both players are striving—as opposed to just hitting the ball around for a while—is a conative activity. If George intends to beat Bill, his Quick Start/Implementor talents will find him all over the court, smashing serves, taking the impossible shot, pulling games out at the last minute. Bill, slightly less a Quick Start with an insistence in Fact Finder, would find George's efforts too fragmented. "He wastes too much energy chasing a ball that is probably going out. He ought to save his effort for more do-able plays," Bill will tell you. Bill has a more strategic sense to his game. He takes the calculated risk. But, for a Fact Finder, his game is as much recreation as George's. If Bill tried to play like George, not only would he have a hard time competing, but the game would stop being recreation for him.

A group vice president of a major American corporation was having trouble accepting such a concept as new as conation, until I guessed his 9 in Fact Finder was sometimes keeping him from resting until it had been satisfied. In front of several of his peers, I told him I bet he did things like crossword puzzles to work off mental energy. I was right. The night before, he told us, he had had difficulty sleeping—until he got up at 2 A.M. and did a couple of crossword puzzles. (He later used the KCI and Job-KCI to help pick his successor.)

If you have unused drive in any Action Mode, it will draw you into activity. Since most people target their strengths on weekday efforts, we think of weekends, especially, as being filled with recreational outlets. But you've undoubtedly had nights when your mind wasn't ready to turn off, and you, like the VP, would be just as well to do something about it.

Because you are likely to commit your strongest modes to income-earning effort, your resistant modes will often be the source of your recreational effort. Unless you're out to win awards for what society has labeled free-time activity, playing your short suits is a good way to keep a balanced hand.

Implementing is one of my short suits, so I have for most of my adult life turned to gardening for recreation. It has renewed me, put me in touch with a part of myself that is usually underground. I can actually feel the tension flow out of me when I garden.

When my children were small, I found myself teaching some basic gardening skills to an after-school class. When the kids' parents came to pick them up, they discovered my unusual hanging floral baskets and wanted to buy them. Soon I was supplying a slew of homes, businesses and restaurants with the fruits of my labor. The Quick Start in me, the entrepreneur, saw lots of business possibilities. Fortunately, even then I think I understood conation on an intuitive level (although I could not yet explain the concept), and I pulled back. Two things were out of whack here. First, while implementing is one of my minor suits, it is not the mode in which I can happily spend the preponderance of my time and energy. Second, if gardening had become a business, I would have been robbed of it as a recreational activity. I needed it as an outlet, not as an income.

In 1985, after my car accident, I spent months in physical therapy. At first, of course, I was unable to work in the garden. When I was sufficiently recovered, I returned to it and found, with a spurt of dismay, that gardening no longer worked for me. I was using up all my Implementor in the reconstructive workouts. I had nothing left for the flowers.

## Leisure: The Absence of Effort

A recent study indicates that Americans, with more leisure than ever before, are finding it more a burden than a blessing. Shorter work weeks, three-day weekends, early retirement, and other occasions for free time are forcing us to learn new coping skills.

Researchers contend that unrealistic expectations make this an emotionally loaded issue. "We are hopelessly trapped," the study reports, "in fantasies about going off to relax and indulge in recreation—sports, the arts, whatever—and returning refreshed and ready to take on the world. Instead, we end up working at our play and returning to our 'real world' more exhausted than ever." The fact is that people have to learn how to enjoy leisure.

It sounds silly to say that we are having trouble having fun. But it gets easier to understand if you take conation into account. Leisure is the non-pursuit of any goal. It's when you go into neutral because your mind has used its conative energy and has earned some downtime. Just as you won't do some things you wish you could, there are things you do for pure pleasure, without any conative striving. Leisure—inactivity—is quite different from recreation. It is the absence of effort, the turning off of your conative system.

Relaxation, or leisure time, comes when you are by yourself or with people who don't expect you to be "on" for them, or to exert energy. Companionship allows for non-energetic meandering, for being together without effort.

Leisure is when you float in the water instead of swimming. It's when you read something with no redeeming value. It's when insistences and resistances don't kick in. Watching the waves hit the beach. Listening to the sound of the birds. Walking aimlessly through the city.

By providing time for taking in sights, sounds, and smells, and for tasting and touching, leisure helps you rejuvenate conatively. To return energized from time off means you've taken time to listen to sounds you wouldn't normally notice or to watch activity that otherwise might not get your attention. The senses don't require museum art or symphonic music, but, the closer you come to natural beauty and honest creativity—works of others' inner spirits—the more your senses will touch and inspire your own creative drives.

Quick Starts are drawn to color—in the art they choose, the clothes they wear, the things they surround themselves with—and a Quick Start will be especially replenished by watching the changing colors of a brilliant sunset. A Fact Finder shows a preference for detail, a need to dress appropriately, and an eye for draftsmanlike perspective, and so can find a special truth in the miniscule drops of dew poised on the complexity of a cobweb. One need do nothing about leisure but be open to it and provide time for it.

One of my children had exhausted himself mentally between a weekend retreat for underclassmen in his high school and studying for exams. When he then tried to start an article for the school newspaper, he found his mind a blank. "I know what I want to write," he said. "I just can't bring myself to do it."

This usually well-disciplined teenager was experiencing exactly the power outage we all face when there's nothing left to give to a project. He could have spent a couple of hours staring at his paper, but he certainly wouldn't have gotten it written. Instead he turned on his stereo full blast (loudness isn't part of the prescription—except at his age) and submerged himself in sound. It did for him what a walk in the woods might do for another. Even the boob tube has its merits when it's not such a regular pastime that it dulls the senses.

Fishing is rekindling for a trade association executive, who makes it clear that he has no intention of actually catching anything. "Putting a line in the water is merely an excuse for enjoying a lazy morning watching the fog lift. If a fish hooks himself, I consider it a nuisance." A few hours without a catch and he's ready to take on the world.

An opera singer was so drained from auditions and performances that she found anything musical impossible for relaxation. She took up stitchery, but, because it was more for relaxation than recreation, she never learned fancy stitches and never framed anything she made.

I love sports as a complete break from what I "do." Don't tell the Phoenix Suns, but I'm not analyzing conative implications when I'm at a game—I'm jumping up and down and screaming my head off, like most spectators who get caught up in it. But, when a team I care about goes to the playoffs, I'm working overtime, figuring out just what they ought to be doing to win. That's when I leave a game feeling like I've just put in a hard day's work.

What about total relaxation, couch-potato time? Anyone can be conatively drained at any time. Staring into space, watching mindless television, absorbing music through the pores instead of the ears, soaking up the sun—why can some people do this and others not? It appears that you have to use up your conative energy before you can relax. It is as difficult to get to this stage when you have pent-up energy as it is to tell the restless toddler on the car trip to just calm down.

People have different friends, with whom they share different kinds of recreational activities, and some with whom they can simply relax and do nothing. An Implementor resistant businessman has several buddies with whom he occasionally plays squash. They all turned out to have quite a bit of Implementor, and are more naturally athletic than him. When the others get together to help each other on home construction projects, they wait and invite him to the party when they are done. They not only recognize his lack of drive to do more than play an occasional game; they accept it. This businessman doesn't talk shop with his friends, but enjoys the opportunity to use his minor mode—a mode in which he normally would not initiate action—or to put forth no energy at all. He is blessed with friends who understand him, and that is not always the case. Some people work well with others but suffer the major malaise of our society—loneliness.

## Acting in Isolation

Life is not a succession of team-building exercises, and certainly not a series of parties or games. Sometimes the relationship that most needs nurturing is your relationship with yourself. Loneliness, as opposed to being alone, is the state of being solitary, left out, alone in a crowd. There are two conative connections to loneliness—cause and effect.

Feelings of loneliness can be caused by not having

someone to do things with. They can also be caused by not having anything to do. It is clear that the cure for loneliness is having somebody to do things with and something to do, which sounds simple enough, but in this world it is easier said than done. We have to put some of our conative energy into combating this pressing social problem, preventing it in our lives and in the lives of others.

Sitting around feeling sorry for yourself gives you reason to be sad. It heightens the sense of inadequacy. Boredom sets in, and you may find yourself becoming listless. Nothing grabs your attention. Nothing spurs you on. Here's the conative solution to loneliness: rather than thinking about it, engage your conative resources. Make a commitment of your mental energy to targeting a solution. Follow your inclinations to do the things that give you the greatest sense of accomplishment. If you have lots of Fact Finder, go to the library and do some research in an area of interest to you. Perhaps there is a problem in your community that could use your help. Become an expert in an area of current concern, and you will be sought out for help. In the process, you may also meet others with similar concerns, and you'll have something in common with them and maybe even find someone with a similar MO.

If Follow Thru is your strength, your best bet for recreational/social activities could be in classes such as design, computer programming, sewing, and so forth. Planning outings for groups or reunions for schoolmates would be the perfect antidote to being alone.

If you have Quick Start energy to burn, do things on the spur of the moment, be spontaneous, try something other than classes or meetings of organizations that may not be open to your need for unique approaches. Do things you've never done before and you'll find others as open to trying the new and different.

Implementor energy often goes into crafts and playing sports, and is generally the easiest to work off after hours. Implementors seem to be less likely to be lonely, because they gravitate to outdoor activities and immerse themselves in projects with plants, animals, or tangible "things." They are interacting, even if it is not with another person.

If your loneliness comes in part from being too tired at the end of the day to go out, these solutions are useless. When lonely nights are brought on by overwhelming days, the answer lies in seeking opportunities for social leisure. Try non-competitive situations, in which people are striving for nothing other than companionship. I've always loved miniature golf, the kind of toy putting green that proves nothing about anyone, except perhaps that they are good sports. That's also why games of chance are so popular for leisure. They don't involve trying—they are just plain fun.

If you don't have the mental energy to go to the meeting, the class, the competition, or anything else, you may just have nothing more to give. Switch to another gear— to a short suit—and you might get a rush of energy. If that doesn't work either, maybe the best thing to do is to do nothing for a while. Just let it happen. Allow yourself a period of renewal. Don't punish yourself with criticism or denial of your natural talents. Give yourself the seventh-inning stretch.

A wonderful man I knew had good reason to be lonely. He had just lost his wife of 55 years. They had been childhood sweethearts, and he was nearly 80. He told me once that people used to comfort him by saying, "You should consider yourself lucky. You were married to Rosie for 55 years." "Yes," he told me. "That's true, but why couldn't I have 56?" Surrounded by children and grandchildren, he felt alone without his wife and dreamed of her every night. But he was never lonely. Busy working, embarking on new projects, learning things every day, seeking out the grandchildren of his friends, to keep in touch with the younger generation. Did he feel sorry for himself? I don't know, but he told me that, alone as he felt, he was never lonely.

Can we expect to have that kind of a love in our lives? Not really, but conation is one factor in our ability to find people to love and be with. It is an important factor, because it determines what you will do about what you feel. By doing what you naturally do, you will find people who appreciate your efforts and will want to do things with you. That's generally how people who fall in love get to know one another.

# – 6 –

# Trusting Another's Instincts

"Ginger Rogers and Fred Astaire had a precision, an instinctive quality between them," Patrick Swayze told *Life* magazine. That's what most people hope for in a relationship.

After a day of consulting for an international trading company, I found myself curious about meeting the owner's wife—his long-suffering wife, in most people's eyes. His KCI result of 5294 hadn't surprised any of the people who work with him, since he's a promoter who's made, lost, and remade a few fortunes; in fact, his associates broke into laughter upon seeing it. "That's him all right," one commented. "He's always coming up with a new angle without concern for all the procedures and regulations involved. He wants it done 'right now,' no matter what. I don't know how his wife puts up with the constant crisis atmosphere he creates."

"Nothing seems to rattle her," his longtime personal assistant told me. Then she explained: "They've lived in five countries and she's usually stayed behind to handle all the details of moving while he's already on to the next place. She entertains on twenty minutes' notice and packs a perfect suitcase in ten. She seems willing to do whatever it takes to help him."

"I think you take unfair advantage of Laren's good nature," chimed in a senior vice-president, looking Conrad right in the eye. "I know, if I pulled the kind of stunts you do, Dot would scalp me alive. And I'd deserve it."

"Thanks a lot, folks," Conrad responded, "Kathy, I want you to meet Laren, so you can see for yourself that I don't abuse my wife."

That afternoon I heard him on the phone asking Laren if she could rearrange her plans so the three of us could go to dinner together. He also congratulated her on finishing some research she was doing for a syndicated columnist, and thanked her for fixing the tape recorder he used during our session.

No, Laren wasn't a 10 in every mode, nor was she a long-suffering wife. She wasn't in conative crisis because of subjugating her needs to her husband's. She was a Facilitator with an MO of 6464, who was finding great satisfaction in accommodating a Quick Start husband, holding a part-time Fact Finder job, and tending to the various needs of three children.

"People miss the point if they think I do what I do because someone else makes me do it," she told me that night. "Conrad needs the limelight and I need to be behind the scenes. I feel a sense of accomplishment without having the stress of being the out-front person. I'm energized by the variety he brings to my life. I never would have done so many interesting things if Conrad hadn't gotten us into them."

Conrad and Laren each willingly fulfilled each other's expectations. He didn't try to push her into starting her own projects, and she didn't resist his need to take on challenges. They did indeed have a precision between them. As she said so well, "We're supporting each other in being who we need to be."

Conative conflict in personal relationships can be alleviated more readily than in the workplace, especially when those involved have a personal commitment to the relationship and a strongly positive affective overlay.

While Laren is a Facilitator who naturally accommodates a variety of activities, many spouses do have to go the extra mile to call on mental energy not automatically accessible. If, as I suspect, the will is powered by the senses, it may be that it's replenished by touching, holding, and the pleasures of sight and sound. This may be a significant factor in making it possible to give more effort than one would in more sterile business or academic environments.

People working on projects or for companies for which they have an emotional attachment or strong belief usually find they have more energy available to give, but these same intents and purposes become even more targeted when someone they love needs their help.

All communication of thought and emotion is made through action. Your conative instincts move you to actually buy the flowers you've been thinking about giving, to fix the broken chair that's been driving him nuts, to reschedule your time so you can be together.

## Making Commitments

Instead of producing conflict between two widely differing MO's, a committed relationship targets talents in mutually supportive ways. Both parties learn to trust the other's instincts and feel free to lean on each other in areas of conative difference.

Personal and business partnerships succeed when both parties have the freedom to be themselves. If either party's needs become subservient to the other's, the conative balance is broken and the commitment is likely to collapse. Overriding affection can keep conative imbalance perched for only so long. Then the persistence of inner striving will cause the tension to surface or the conflicts to go to the combustion stage.

David (8723) and Sharon (8543) had been married for ten years and had two boys, aged 5 and 7. Their MO's weren't so different that they would normally have had problems working things out, but David had committed most of his energy to his engineering job and came home drained many weeknights. On weekends he played what he considered well-earned rounds of golf. That used up his recreational time and energy. A concerned father, he set aside what he thought was quality time for his kids— which was really only the Implementor energy he had left over to build a fort or teach them to ride a bike. He rarely read to them or joined them in other kinds of activities, because he'd already done enough Fact Finder work at the office to exhaust the energy he'd need to answer all the questions they'd invariably ask.

By the time David and Sharon had a moment alone together, she had also drained her resources. As a law professor, she typically spent hours every evening preparing for the next day's classes. Trying to be the perfect wife and mother, she read stacks of child-rearing books, evaluated school activities, budgeted household expenses, scheduled dentist's appointments, and planned nutritious meals. No one could fault her for trying. But her commitment to her primary relationship with David was insufficient to preserve energy for the moments they had together.

She was too tired for sex, and he wasn't willing to make it a priority if she showed so little interest. He was too drained to act with enthusiasm when she fixed a special meal, so she quit bothering. He began coming home from the office too late to have dinner with her and the family.

The conative and affective are so intertwined that a lack of doing things together can cause a loss of love. Absence may make the heart grow fonder, but it also opens the door for problems. The best way to grow apart is to *be* apart, which can, of course, happen even when you're in the same room. David and Sharon were so busy being good professionals and parents that they had become lousy lovers—and not even very good friends.

Committed relationships don't have to be marriages. Some friendships are of the do-anything-for-each-other variety. It doesn't take a trauma for such friends to appear—they set aside time and energy to be with you, even if it's by long-distance phone calls. Friendships require mutual effort, too. But, because most people aren't willing to go through as much tension or conflict in friendships, less-committed social relationships are generally either with conatively similar people, or with special-situation friends with whom you have recreational outlets in a particular mode. For instance, the Fact Finder/Quick Start businessman whose friends were often Implementors with whom he played sports, or a 8615 doctor who enjoys having a couple of Quick Start friends stop by with zany ideas for things to do.

Bill and Sue also had quite different conative profiles. From similar backgrounds, they'd gone to the same college, read the same books, and shared politics, religion, and a general view of life. But Sue was an insistent Quick Start with moderate Fact Finder; Bill was an insistent Fact Finder with solid Follow Thru. One of their most important bonds was Implementor resistance—they were confirmed couch-potatoes, and both loved games. Sue's favorite was Scrabble, and, as a Quick Start, she beat Bill every time. Bill chose gin rummy. As a Fact Finder, Bill whipped Sue consistently. So they stopped playing games.

When they entertained, Sue took great pride in making everything happen perfectly, at the last minute and against all odds. Bill worked out his anxiety over her slap-dash approach by cleaning the top of the refrigerator just as the company was due. She cooked, he cleaned up. Bill's Implementor was even worse than Sue's. He hired people to do the handywork (Sue, who was resistant to Follow Thru, would never schedule to call anybody to fix anything), and, to Sue's delight, took care of the household details. Sue held the map when they went on car trips.

Even with such different MO's, they had four significant ingredients for a successful relationship: love, commitment, equality, and trust in each other's instincts. They were also two people who were secure in themselves, who were fulfilling their personal destinies and therefore didn't need to impinge on each other's freedom to be themselves.

Trusting another person's instincts is required in committed relationships, whether it's a police officer trusting that her partner will check a situation out thoroughly or an aerial artist trusting his partner's timing on a catch, a business person trusting the intuition of his out-of-town partner in cutting a deal, or a woman trusting her date not to take her sailing if he can't handle the boat. Having confidence in each other's inclinations allows each partner to benefit from the other's unharnessed creative power. Lack of such trust undermines the relationship and the partners' ability to function interdependently. The most important mode to trust another in is usually the most difficult one in which to give sway, as it's the one in which you may resist and on which the other person insists.

A Quick Start insistent man convinced his resistant Quick Start girlfriend to trust him in last-minute switches in their vacation plans. The girlfriend figured that, while they never seemed to end up doing what was originally scheduled, they'd always found interesting adventures, so she opted out of the decisions. Her confidence in his forte was rewarded both in her not having to exert her limited energy for such things, and in the relationship benefitting from the proven trust.

Your MO is your natural advantage, a resource you bring to a relationship. Whether bartering it, as discussed in earlier chapters, or committing it unequivocally, it is the most significant asset you have to offer.

Why would a person not openly and freely give his or her conative talents to a relationship? The following affective problems stem from conative causes:

## THREATS TO RELATIONSHIPS

- *Guilt* over the imperfection of not being a 10 in every mode.
- *Fear* of strengths being rejected or resistances ridiculed.
- *Pressure* to change how he or she acts.
- *Insecurity* over comparative value of knacks.
- *Avoidance* of conative conflict.

These threats exist no matter what the MOs of those involved.

There's a bittersweet response when one person in a relationship is at either extreme in a mode. Whether it's 1 or 2 units or 9 or 10, the difference from the norm is so great that some suffering will likely take place. A 10 in any talent can wish at times to not stand out so much. Acceptance and support in persisting in the march to a different drummer is a true measure of love, especially when society tends to covet conformity. Eccentricity is usually considered fine in the elderly, who apparently are deemed either sufficiently harmless or deserving of such a posture. But people are wary of the young upstart who thinks he has to do everything his own way.

It takes a lot of love to disregard your Follow Thru spouse's insistence on replacing everything you put down so it's in its proper place, or not to cajole an Implementor into discussions she would normally avoid, or to listen to the irrelevant blow-by-blow experiences of a Fact Finder. If what is being dished out isn't your cup of tea, it can be downright frustrating to have to face it day in, day out—unless you take joy in the other person's successes, are accepting of the genuine need from which it stems, and have a sense of humor about the absolute hopelessness of ever trying to do anything to change the other person's conative nature.

Some highly insistent people report a real relief when they discover someone who can go toe-to-toe with them in a Fact Finder battle of minutiae, or in wilderness hikes, or whatever the shared inclination. The two can maximize recreational outlets, even if friends and family may be worn down by their unrelenting correction of each other's stories, or their endurance climbs. They pace each other in uncanny ways, like Dr. Reid, whose husband can give an hour-long presentation on a photo slide of their vacation the same way she does when lecturing on a bacterial slide for her classes.

When two people are insistent in one mode but have differing resistances, I hear a lot more confusion over expectations—and often the defensiveness caused by the guilt of what they won't do. Hal (4286) and Jean (5681) say their attraction came through the shared need for Quick Start activities. Both had come out of first marriages to resistant Quick Starts and recognized spontaneity as an essential ingredient to a future relationship. When these unbridled Quick Starts discovered how much they had in common, they married in a ceremony that accommodated their parents' sense of tradition, but without giving anyone much notice.

When, on their island honeymoon, Jean wanted to stay inside to finish writing thank-you notes, Hal couldn't believe it. "Some free spirit you are," he told her. "You're more chained to convention than you realize."

She was locked into her own MO, Quick Start *and all*. She could no more enjoy a trip until most of the loose ends were tied up than he could stay tied up indoors. But they were just married and didn't want to be apart, so they came up with a division of labor, where he did the folding, stamping, and addressing and she did the writing. That wasn't a bad use of his Implementor, but it was obviously a compromise for him.

Years later, after finding out about the conative connection, he described the mistake he had made when he took her on a honeymoon adventure he was sure she would enjoy. "I wanted her to finish her stupid notes so we could get out in the boat I'd rented and go exploring an uninhabited island. She went along with it because I was so enthusiastic. But, once we were on the island and it started to rain and all our stuff got soaked and there were bugs and I'd forgotten the drinks, it was no longer her idea of fun. It was a disaster. I thought she'd deceived me about who she was."

What he hadn't seen was her resistance to physical risks in comparison to his gravitation toward them. He hadn't recognized that her spontaneity was tempered by a need to plan for contingencies and to have explanations. Her form of risk-taking was more theoretical, on paper, than his, out amongst the bugs and bushes. She was nonplussed when Hal hadn't checked the weather forecast and had caused the mess they were in.

"If we'd known about the conative connection, it would have saved us a lot of frustration," she said. Actually, probably not. These two are basically trial-and-error types whose different ways of approaching risk will never change. Frustration will abound, but at least now they know why.

Since Hal won't sit still for the conclusive conversation Jean requires, I recommended that she work it through in her own mind until she can make her points concisely. Rather than setting aside a specific time just to talk, it works best to do it while they're doing something else together, like driving, walking, fixing a meal, or cleaning the house. "It's less oppressive that way." he says.

When they decided to stop smoking, Jean was frustrated that Hal wouldn't commit to going to a class. He was going to cold-turkey it, but she'd tried that before and knew it wouldn't work for her. She had to ease off, following a regimen. I got them to turn it into a contest, the ultimate means of engaging most Quick Starts. Knowing that he'd require tactile substitutes for holding a cigarette in his hand and that she'd demand more of a system for her countdown, I suggested that she design a chart that monitored their efforts and that he select tangible rewards they'd give each other. It worked. When they were completely off cigarettes, her reward was her Quick Start success in beating her own "straw man" system. He, of course, ignored the system as part of the challenge.

## Attractions and Distractions

Having observed hundreds of couples over the years, I have found that those who remarry or marry for the first time later in life tend to marry those conatively similar. Spending time doing things together recreationally seems to be a driving force in making the marital choice. On the other hand, people who marry when they are young usually have differing MOs. It seems people attract others who complement their strengths and can provide needed talents during the nest-building years. Having a spouse who can fix anything is a great attraction for a klutz. A lover who brings new experiences into your life can fore-tell a lifetime of serendipity you may otherwise have missed. Yet the conative contrasts that bring synergy to relationships are at the root of many marital conflicts.

An 8822 husband was concerned that a house be an excellent investment, be appropriate to his status in life, have lots of space for bookshelves, fit in well with the neighborhood, and not require much upkeep. His 4385 wife had fallen in love with a house that had a serene garden that she promised would be her responsibility. It only had two bedrooms, which was all they needed, but which made it risky in his eyes because of resale problems. She loved the uniqueness of it; he said it would be impossible to get a good appraisal on it.

When there's conative conflict between marriage partners it can enhance the union by bringing different work-related activities and recreational outlets to the table, but they need a home that melds those differences into an environment with a sense of unity.

In this case, the wife used her Quick Start to sell her husband on the idea that they could eventually add a room that would serve as his library and fill the resale need for a third bedroom. She used her Implementor to make a model that demonstrated exactly how it could be done without destroying the integrity of the house design, which would naturally concern him. She was willing to be flexible about putting books in the dining room in the meantime. His compromise was to set a figure that an appraisal had to meet, and to make a commitment to the house if it came in at that amount. He also wanted assurances that he would not be expected to lay a hand on the room-addition project.

If your significant other is significantly different from you conatively, you don't need to be driven to distraction; the natural conflict can be a plus in the relationship.

A 3394 fell in love with a 7553 who was willing to "cover" for her on the record-keeping details of his job. A 5761 believes his 8237 girlfriend can do anything because she does everything he won't do of his own volition. Common goals provide outlets for differing talents and a mutual dependency can foster a special closeness.

It is essential for you to be equals in the relationship, or one person's needs will be overpowering. Your conation is how you respond to the world around you, and that can be shared but never set above others' conation. Still, just because you're conative equals doesn't mean it's easy to give others as much credit for their way of working as you give yourself for yours. Nor does it help when wrongly conceived role models or self-help books would have you believe you could have had—or can create—a lover who is a perfect 10 in every mode.

Ruth and Robert are considered by many to be one of the oddest of couples. He's a 2495 and she's a 7823. They're from different socio-economic groups, different religions, and different regions, and have very different personalities. She's very self-assured and assertive and he's an introvert with a lot of insecurities. How do you suppose they've stayed together for so many years? Yes, their sexual relationship is apparently terrific. And, yes, he introduces a variety of sexual and social activities into her life. But it goes much beyond that.

While he dabbles in selling oddities of various types and changes career paths several times a year, including starting a variety of companies that never really get off the ground, she brings in a consistent income. He appreciates the mortgage getting paid, and she loves the social events that take place when he does happen to close a deal. While he complains that she makes him justify everything he does, he recognizes that he can continue to experiment with an assortment of projects only because she keeps him away from the worst of the lot.

"Knowing the inevitability of how he's going to act lets me relax and enjoy the fun times rather than always worrying about how it will turn out," she told me. "Our energies aren't going into trying to figure out why or finding a way to change one another. We marvel in what fun it is to be so different and yet have this unifying thing called a sense of purpose."

Catering to a loved one's conative needs is a sign of true understanding. In *Fear of Flying*, Erica Jong's heroine complains that her husband never speaks to her when they are making love. For an Implementor, touch is the crucial thing. If you love a Fact Finder, though, hunt up some poetry to put what's in your heart into words, because that will matter enormously. The crucial mix is one between conation and affection. Consideration helps you operate in your partner's insistent mode for the moment, and accommodation allows you to put all of your energy into making love.

It's not impossible to go into your own short suits to act as a companion for someone else. Ever seen a spouse reading a book at a football game? That's a conative compromise. If a wife uses her smidge of Quick Start in adding her husband's three unexpected guests for dinner, he could return the favor by summoning up his tad of Implementor to massage her back after the party is over. When a resistent Follow Thru repeats a lesson over and over for a handicapped spouse, that's a sign of true devotion.

While we give of ourselves in personal relationships, it isn't possible to sacrifice yourself completely, to deplete all your conative energy in the service of another. Each individual has the need to persevere in his or her own being, and it makes no more sense to betray yourself than to deny another person.

For couples who conflict more than they coincide, it takes special effort to keep things going over time. But there are ways to make it work.

• Set goals that require joint participation. Self-reliance is out of place in this kind of cooperative effort.
• Put the party on together. Build or decorate the addition to your house together.
• Jointly help a friend or neighbor through a trauma.
• Pick a goal that is important enough to both of you, so that it won't be set aside easily, but make sure that it is not so far off that the relationship won't last long enough to see the goal accomplished (like raising kids).

You have to make an effort to stay in touch with friends, and you have to commit to a relationship every bit of yourself—not only your feelings but your conative self as well. What we've called thoughtfulness requires conative commitment to action—it's really *do*-fulness.

A dominant Follow Thru told me she won't continue dating a man who says all the right things but shows up late or calls for a date at the last minute. An Implementor said purchased gifts didn't mean much to him; he considers it a real commitment when someone handcrafts something for him, or picks a flower from her own garden.

Through their conative selves, couples build nests together, raise kids, entertain, share recreational activities. These activities keep people together long after the wine-and-roses period is over.

## Compatibility or Complacency?

If your personal partner is your conative clone, things may look dandy to begin with. Your standard operating procedures make the relationship look trouble-free. Implementors in love might hike, climb mountains, make pottery together, or understand the beauty of massage. Quick Starts improvise together and don't mind the mutual interruptions and distractions. Fact Finders are pleased to find another person who can be as interested in this subject or that issue as long as they are, a mate who doesn't tap her toe while the family tree is being traced at yet another social gathering. Follow Thrus together understand the beauty of immaculately organized closets and always doing the laundry on Mondays. Neither would object to annually scheduling their vacation for the same two weeks in July at the same neat and tidy resort.

But if your personal partner is your conative clone, you can stagnate. Because conation is not inherited, children usually inject conative differences into your lives, but, unless their needs are given equal status, they may add tension rather than synergy. A couple who both lead with Fact Finder and Follow Thru have a son with the proclivities of a Quick Start/Implementor. Their lives have been enhanced by the adventures they have taken with this three-year-old. His needs have found them going places they never would have gone and, meeting people they never would have met.

Conatively cloned couples can seek out friends and relatives who add differing dimensions to their lives. A favorite uncle brings Fact Finder into one household. "He keeps us informed," his niece told me. "We get a lot out of his backgrounding us before a special election, for instance. We never talk about world events when he's not around. He keeps us in touch with all that."

Because conative cloning causes inertia, it keeps people on the same plateau. Just as it obstructs productivity in the workplace, it can lead to sameness in lifestyles. Unlike conflict, which draws attention to itself, forcing something to be done about it, the complacency of cloning often causes hidden problems.

"I can't do what you do, but I love to hear how you do it." Taking an interest in how others achieve adds secondary experiences that keep your own experience fresh and invigorating. Getting overly caught up in your own activities, especially if you have a conatively compatible spouse, can be stultifying.

Donna, a young wife with Follow Thru strength in common with her husband, told me: "We have the same friends, like to do the same things on weekends, and are very consistent in how we handle the kids. Our relationship gives me a lot of security and a sense of complete compatibility. Sure it would be fun sometimes to be with someone who surprises me once in a while, but I'm in a very comfortable place."

That's the story I tend to hear from people in long-term relationships with conative closeness, unless they are trying to work together or managing difficult family problems. If there is a trauma, two resistant Quick Starts would miss a partner who's good in a crisis. Without Follow Thru both parties could be hoping the other would handle the intricacies of a move. Mutual resistances are always more difficult to resolve than insistences.

If your primary relationship has neither the conflict of extremely different MOs nor the potential inertia of similarities, there is the opportunity to meet on common ground. Meeting where you accommodate may not be that easy, because insistences are your most obvious traits—second only to resistances. But find that common ground, because it may be the source of long and happy years with someone you love.

## Confronting Expectations

Nancy and Bob found their marriage on the rocks when Bob began having an affair with a business associate. Nancy had been Bob's bookkeeper for the first ten years that he was in business for himself. She was exactly what he needed—precise, efficient, thorough (6833). At home, of course, she was the same. The house was kept in order. The family finances were well documented.

Nancy took enormous pride in her MO. She congratulated herself on being a superb manager in years when money had been tight, on setting aside savings for their retirement, on having a beautifully kept home. While she didn't have words to describe her resistance to Quick Start, she recognized her pattern of needing security. She had thought her antipathy for anything that required physical problem-solving arose because she was a girl, not because she was resistant to Implementor. Her husband, Bob, was a technician (6257) who had tried to run a small manufacturing business after his partner had died. Nancy filled in the gaps in his competence. He was often at the office for fourteen hours at a time, and appreciated coming home to a smooth-running home.

When his company was acquired, Bob stayed on as president, but it no longer required as much of his energy. Suddenly, he found himself with shorter work days, less fulfillment, more money, and serious marital conflicts.

The orderly running of the household, when he was spending more time there, became too orderly. Nancy was still managing the family finances with the care she had always exercised. But now Bob was in a mood to spend. He was bored with his work, uneasy with the tight structure of the larger company, and ready to try his hand at something else. Nancy, on the other hand, was annoyed with the tools he left lying around and the equipment he kept dragging into the house. And she was troubled by the realization that suddenly the rules of the marriage had changed.

The conative profiles that had been complementary in the early years of their marriage, that had allowed the two to work as a team when they were building the business and their family nest, were now a source of conflict. Because they no longer trusted each other's instincts, it was impossible for either one of them to accommodate the other, certainly not in the Follow Thru or Implementor modes. Their best chance for a meeting of the minds was to use the one strong suit they had in common, Fact Finder, to evaluate the situation and seek appropriate solutions.

Most marriage counselors would be confronting the issue of feelings. Did they care enough to compromise? How strong was the love between them? But the crisis in this marriage arose from the differences in the way Nancy and Bob *acted*, and their need to find ways to make those differences work in their personal partnership. It was a conative conflict. But, without the appropriate vocabulary, Bob and Nancy had difficulty communicating what was happening to them and how they felt about it.

Communication depends on symbols—words, gestures— and, until now, people have not had the words, the terminology, the concepts needed to explain a problem like Nancy's and Bob's.

Their marriage counselor did indeed get them talking about feelings. After half a dozen sessions that went round and round, Bob got disgusted with making lists of all the good things in their life and all the bad. The bottom line was that he didn't see a light at the end of the tunnel. He found solace in an affair.

When Nancy learned what was going on and confronted him, he spoke of the new relationship as one in which he felt appreciated for who he was without being criticized for it. This was his conative self crying out for acknowledgment. Bob found no personal fulfillment in his financial gains. Dozens of my upper-income-bracket clients have attested to the fact that material rewards cannot satisfy intrinsic needs. A person's proudest accomplishment is rarely tied to money.

Given a new understanding of the difference between affective and conative needs, Bob and Nancy have been able to communicate their individual pain and their need for each other. They have begun the search for compromise and enhancement of each other. That doesn't mean there won't be problems in the future. But at least they'll have a basis for working them out—if they choose to.

Confronting expectations may help us see when they are conatively absurd; when no one could—or would want to—live up to our idea of perfection.

"Joe built me my dream house, but he's not once sent me a romantic letter."

"Ralph is very dependable and efficient at everything he does, but I wish once in a while he'd surprise me, sweep me off on some unplanned adventure."

"Darlene's terrific at digging out the facts, but I wish she'd learn when to quit."

"Louise is always willing to go along with whatever I suggest, but I'd love it if she'd initiate more activities."

A husband can work fourteen-hour days, do the dishes after dinner, run errands, cook if he's home first, and yet, if he doesn't retile the bathroom himself, his wife thinks he is lazy. Without the concept of conation to explain why he resists working with his hands, he may also castigate himself for his perceived imperfections.

Culturally defined expectations and sexist assumptions have wives carrying out Follow Thru roles and husbands having to be macho Implementors or, at the very least, expert Fact Finders. Since there are no differences in the distribution of each mode between the sexes, lots of people are put in the wrong stereotype.

## Timing Is Everything

A committed relationship that requires working to-gether—whether to raise a family, build a house, or run a business—will complicate conative issues, because the two people in it are interacting on so many levels. They have shared commitments to their primary relationship and other goal-directed striving, they interact recreationally, and are probably companions in leisure. That's a lot to ask of a relationship when all those responses are otherwise available from a variety of sources.

Is it too much to ask? Yes, if you expect your mate to alter his or her strengths to meet your needs. Just because you're ready for some Quick Start recreation, don't expect the spouse handling a crisis with the community project to be able to drudge up more of the pioneering spirit.

If one partner needs mental downtime and the other has been bored out of his or her brain, the levels of intensity will be as out of sync as the modes in which they're operating. When that happens, there's no use badgering one to calm down and the other to get involved. Here again conation and time converge. Timing marital activity, from making love to serving leftovers, is integral to the response you receive.

At the end of the day, Clay (7364), who sells insurance, figures that he shouldn't have to use up his slight Follow Thru keeping track of his kids' schedules, or even his own and his wife's social plans. His wife, Susan, does all that. Because she spends the week—and many evenings—cooking for her catering business, she is altogether empty of Implementor in free time, which is why she leaves the yard work to Clay. At the moment, Clay is draining his Quick Start and Fact Finder on the job. Some evenings he'll read or play Trivial Pursuit with the kids. But he'd rather watch TV.

Susan (6464), a Facilitator, keeps track of inventory, checks her records before turning them over to her book-keeper, and pores over recently published cookbooks in search of new dishes. Her Fact Finder is down to the last drop and she does not join in Trivial Pursuit. Her partner is a strong Follow Thru, which leaves Susan able to use hers to keep track of the family schedule and let Clay off that hook. Her Quick Start is put to use, for the most part, in connection with their three children, who are all very different and who require her to shift gears with great frequency.

How does a family like this share free time? If one or more of the children is Implementor insistent, they might work with their mother in the kitchen or help their father in the yard—more than just when they're told to. Clay's home chores and Susan's work are not going to leave much Implementor left for softball with the kids.

On vacations, of course, that might all change. Then Susan might play Trivial Pursuit and Clay might plan the sightseeing. Being out of character once in a while confuses anyone who doesn't understand the way we trade off our energies, but it can recharge your batteries like nothing else in the world.

If each person's conative capacities are recognized and respected, sharing work can be every bit as gratifying and as affectively positive as sharing recreation and leisure. Only when work is violating the essential person, is demanding of energy that is not available, does it create tension that is counterproductive. The same tension that permeates some workplaces exists in many homes. It comes from unrealistic demands—from yourself and from others. Just as you would guard against an intrusion into your home or a violation of your body, it is essential to protect your mental resources. That means keeping an inventory of what you have left to give, being realistic about what you can do, and letting yourself off the hook once in a while. If you can do those three things for the person you love, then you both have a shot at proving you can make it work.

# – 7 –

# Nurturing the Will

Carolyn's announcement to her family that she intended to go to art school aroused a storm of protests. Art was a nice hobby—a very fine hobby, actually—but not a *career*. In her family, a career was medicine, or teaching, or research.

When Richard was born, his mother worked hard to be sure Richard wouldn't be as set in his ways as his dad. The mobile over the crib was changed every week, his baby bed was out in different spots in the room, he was taken to a variety of places and fed at various times. His mother never connected Richard's frequent agitation to such disruptions. In fact, she was shocked when I suggested she might be creating tension for the baby. Perhaps Richard's instinct for Follow Thru was as strong as his father's. If so, his mother wasn't going to change it by keeping him in perpetual motion. When she stopped trying to make her child less structured, Richard's tension and frustration abated.

It's bad enough not to build on the benefits of managing conative traits in the workplace. It's a devastating indictment that our schools restrict the use of creative instincts. But the greatest damage to human potential comes from parents who do not nurture a child's will.

You don't have to have children to gain insight from a discussion of the conative connection in a family. It can help you understand—even forgive—your parents, your siblings, and those neighbors who don't seem to be able to control their kids.

Focusing on conative characteristics unobscured by the baggage of adulthood helps us consider how early a child is burdened with expectations for how he or she *ought* to act. Confidence is chipped away from the first moment a child is punished for doing what comes naturally.

Parents don't teach a child to be conative. They don't control his innate capabilities which, indeed, only respond to self-control. He comes into the world testing his will, which is fully developed at birth and ready to have its way. What takes place at home can both foster and validate the creative powers of family members. Or it can thwart them, and cause tension. Contests of will leave no victors. But they do leave scars.

When families understand that conation is instinctive and immutable, they will save themselves enormous stress and their loved ones great pain. To know, or to sense, that something integral to your self is felt to be unacceptable to the people you love can cut deeply and undermine self-confidence. The challenge for parents is to teach a child to commit his or her talents to good purposes and to be able to work with others to achieve greater goals.

If Richard's mother can accept her husband, can't she also accept her child? If Carolyn doesn't view her family as philistines, can't they learn to accept her art?

A family that is whole (to use psychological jargon) doesn't necessarily have to have every member home for the holidays, write round-robin letters, or stay with the tradition of grandmother's meatloaf every Wednesday night. A healthy family is one in which the members *know* each other, *care* about each other and *act* accordingly.

## Taking Kids as They Come

Families often come in a conative mix, because conation doesn't appear to be genetic. Support for differing abilities becomes the hallmark of a healthy home. I was impressed when a young man applying for a job with me said he could put up with my Quick Start insistence as opposed to his mild accommodation in the mode because he had a Quick Start father whom he had learned to appreciate—and who had fortunately never imposed his style on his son.

When friends become like family, it means that they have accepted you, and you them, for who you are—with all your insistences, resistances, and conative imperfections. But there is no surer way for a family member to be made to feel like an outsider than to be treated as though they aren't doing things "the way we Johnsons do them."

The Johnsons are an outdoorsy bunch who go camping and fishing and play all sorts of sports. The eldest son,

John, is a tackle on the high school football team. June is a good all-round athlete who, at eleven, came in second in the state junior swimming championships. But Jeff is eight and a klutz. He's too resistant in Implementor to have much dexterity, and too resistant in Quick Start to be competitive. He would rather just stay inside and read.

The Johnsons assume that Jeff hasn't found his sport yet. They come up with statements like "Wait till he hits his stride." Or, "Hey, Jeff, you'll show us all up one of these days." Jeff longs to be accepted by this affectionate group. He knows he's loved, but he also hears the message that he's supposed to be more like the rest of them.

Jeff may well develop better small-muscle control and outgrow his clumsiness; he may even find a sport he can reasonably call his own. Will Jeff have the drive to win athletic competitions, even though he isn't a natural? Could be. Many of the professional athletes I've known have Jeff's Fact Finder/Follow Thru MO. They play a consistently strategic game and effectively target their energy. But Jeff will only accomplish this when he commits himself to the goal. He can be coerced to play, but he can't be compelled to win.

If Jeff had been born with the Implementor knack, he still might not have been an outdoorsy type. Not all Implementors play sports. The Johnsons might have worried he was wasting his talent, but he could have applied it to a musical interest (in all probability, a percussion instrument), or art (sculpture, no doubt). Conative knack can cover a multitude of interests and activities.

Since everyone is equal in mental energy or conative talent, all members of a family or any other group have just as much potential for—and are equally far away from—

perfection. Jeff Johnson isn't being belligerent when he doesn't pick up the ball to play—he's being himself. His hope of overcoming the family conative bias rests heavily on his ability to let his parents and siblings know who he is and how he feels. That ability, in turn, depends on how comfortable he *feels* saying such things, and how well he's being *taught* to communicate. The three parts of the mind are so interdependent that it could take Jeff years to distinguish how he feels from what he is willing to say and do about it.

## Fostering Success

Encouraging individuality, letting children know there is no one right way to accomplish anything, offering options—these are the keys to good parenting. But it's tough to do, especially when you have learned that there is a right and the wrong way for you. It helps when parents see their own MOs as contrasting with their children's and recognize the validity of the differences. Do you remember any of these from your childhood?:

"Why do you always have to do it your own way?"
"Why won't you just let me show you?"
"What makes you think you can do it?"
"When are you going to stop being like that?"
"Why won't you just try it?"

Those aren't questions—they're accusations, and it makes some grown-ups flinch just to hear them again. People who recognize that no one can be a 10 in every mode make better parents. I'd even go so far as to say they make better people: better adjusted, better equipped to deal with problems, better judges of others, better at laughing at their own and others' foibles. The humor people need may even be self-deprecating, a realization that quirks need not be shared as long as they are accepted, and, as parents, this ability to recognize their own idiosyncracies and the difference of their kids goes very far toward allowing their children to be themselves.

Even if a child hasn't put his talents to the best use, these statements attack his sense of self-worth. If parents can substitute another kind of question, kids can relax and learn to do it their own way.

"Would you like to see how I do it?"
"Do you have a way that might work better?"
"Would you like to try?"
"What would you do differently?"
"Why is it your way just doesn't work for me?"

Parents must overcome personal conative biases, those of childcare specialists, of the education system, of grandparents—even of friends and neighbors—to assure they're giving children both the free rein they need and sufficient guidance. Those parents who trust their instincts—and those of their children—seem always to do best.

## Letting Kids Play Their Own Game

We often undermine youngsters' talents, even though our purpose is to nurture them. "What do you mean you rearranged the shelves. You're supposed to be getting ready for the dance." "Get off your rear end, put your pens away and get out there and play ball with the other kids!" And we sometimes lose the trust of our kids in the process.

One of the most talented young artists I know was belittled by his father. Dad was a real-estate developer who had made good money through Quick Start hustle. He *knew* that the way to get ahead in this world was by having a lot of irons in the fire and knocking on new doors every day. The boy resisted both Quick Start and Implementor, and his work had the intrinsic style of the Follow Thru/ Fact Finder. The father continually berated him for being too lazy to play in sports or get real jobs. That the boy was commissioned for illustrations before he had graduated from high school didn't count. He wasn't doing things Dad's way.

The boy was completely miserable. All the praise in the world from his teachers and clients could not replace what he so desperately needed from his father. This conative problem spilled over into a lack of confidence in his own talents and a lack of respect for his father, because of his insensitivity. Only years later when the young man was winning major art contests did his father come around. But, by then, it was too late. His son didn't even invite him to his first one-man show.

"Why did you *do* that?" a father shrieked at his active, Quick Start/Implementor child as she ducked behind a display in the grocery store, knocking down dozens of Ritz cracker boxes. As he collared the kid, I wanted to collar him. "Find outlets for her curiosity, don't clobber her for it," I wanted to say. But he was off on his tirade: "I've told you a thousand times not to touch things. Curiosity killed the cat, you know. You're a naughty girl. You don't care what I say. I don't know what I'm going to do with you."

Even if he had had exactly the same conative profile as his child, he might still have been embarrassed by her. As an adult he would have learned to control some of the impulses she used flat out. But in this case he had no empathy for her whatsoever. If he had understood her conative needs, he might have had her run off some of that energy before going shopping, helping her discover how to use her talents in more constructive ways. Of course, getting rattled in supermarkets by your toddler isn't strictly a conative problem, as any parent can tell you. But, after you go home, and no longer can see the looks you got at the check-out counter, maybe a smile or a laugh could erupt—when you recognize that the toddler is acting true to form.

## Realistic Expectations

No matter how eager we are as parents to recognize the individuality of each child, and to foster that unique person, many barriers stand in our way. Our own habits and, the expectations of our friends, relatives, and society at large make us want our kids to conform to all kinds of expectations—not only in performance, but in style. While we can't change the basic nature of our children, we can change unrealistic expectations. Here are some mental sets to recognize in yourself and to stop when you feel them coming on:

**If It Worked for Me It'll Work for You:** A great many parents share the misconception that what has brought them fulfillment will do the same for their child. But the only thing that will bring a sense of accomplishment to their children is the same freedom to be themselves that the parents enjoyed.

There are many versions. Your father was an accountant. He badgered you into following in his footsteps. You did, but you hated every day of it. Your son will *not* be an accountant. But maybe he is perfectly suited to do that work. Forcing him away from it is as destructive as forcing you into it was.

OR: Your daughter has always been an excellent student, a fine writer, a good storyteller. She's always been a bit absent-minded, though. Forgetful. Messy. Not very well organized. But now she's married and expecting a baby. Naturally, you think, now she'll change. She'll have to grow up, get her act together ("get your act together" is too often a euphemism for "act more like me"), learn to plan ahead, and schedule her time.

Of course your daughter won't change. She will mother in her own way, just as she studies, writes, or works. Not understanding your daughter's conative differences, you may see this "refusal" to change as a personal rejection. "Wasn't I a good mother? Then why don't you do it the way I did?" Parents can teach values, but they can't instill the methods to carry them out.

**Do as I Say, Not as I Did:** Because they feel unhappy with their lot in life and are sure that some specific change would have made the difference (more education, different education, more money, less money, more travel, fewer upheavals, and so on) some parents try to dissuade children from following in their footsteps.

This is the mirror image of the first example. It is saying "Do as I didn't", and can take many forms. "Get good grades. I wasted school by putting my energy into sports." "You must have a specific job skill, because I had trouble getting a job as a generalist." "You must learn to do home repairs because I've spent a fortune having to hire someone to do it."

Whether any of these conative demands are right—and some could be—they're made for the wrong reasons and have a negative effect.

**You'll Never Get Better at It if You Don't Try:** Many parents believe they're doing a youngster a favor by forcing him into the very activities he tries to avoid. While it's possible for any person to do whatever has to be done, the art of parenting is to get them done through use of natural talents. "You must learn to finish what you start." Why? If you're resistant to Follow Thru you're wasting your time and energy to tie everything up just for the sake of completion when you could be doing something else. (You can tell your mother I said so.)

Save your breath instead of telling a Quick Start who is also resistant in Fact Finder not to try anything silly. Don't tell an Implementor kid not to touch, or a Fact Finder to hurry up and decide even though he doesn't know what he's getting into. If a child resists taking chances there's no amount of cajoling that will turn him into a risk taker. As in the studies that show we're better off listening to our bodies when it comes to what we eat or how much we sleep, we are coming to know that listening very carefully to our children's instincts is the best form of nurturing.

**Go Where the Opportunities Are:** Instead of going with their instincts, kids are often encouraged to follow social or economic trends or opportunities. As the financial strains grew in the farm belt, the Bryants told their kids not to consider working the land, even though, for at least one of them, it was the natural choice.

In the fifties, when the Russians sent up Sputnik, the smart money was on pushing your kid into math and science. Many "gifted" programs still insist that kids score high in Fact Finder to be eligible for the classes, thereby cutting out much conative talent. Parents often buy into the educational scam—better college opportunities, better access to high-paying jobs—but it doesn't necessarily lead to the betterment of their children.

**It's Not in the Cards:** Limiting expectations can take many forms. "No one in our family could ever hope to be. . . . We're too. . . ." Or the equally harmful "Why would someone from our family even consider doing that?"

Marianne's family has an academic tradition that made her take for granted that she would end up with a graduate degree. After getting her first PhD. she discovered how little it meant to her and how unsatisfied she felt. So, of course, she thought she could fill the void by going for another PhD. On the heels of her second post-graduation, she took the KCI, breaking into tears when she saw the results. "You have to be kidding! I'm a 9 in Quick Start and only a 2 in Fact Finder? Finally, I know I'm not crazy. I'm just trying too hard to be what the tribe told me I should be."

Because she felt she was not supposed to show her family what was inside, she moved across the country from them as a conative compromise. "What they don't know won't hurt them," she said, as she looked for a job in sales.

There are, of course, the proverbial ethnic stereotypes and sexual misconceptions: girls can't do math, boys are better at shop, men can't nurture small children, and women can't manage each other. None of these has a grain of truth. Correcting a single misconception removes the greatest obstacle to effective parenting. It is that children don't *become* who they will be, they come as who they are.

## Finding Common Ground

When our knack isn't compatible with our child's, one of the best alternatives is to find a mentor with a matching MO. Maybe Grandpa will take the kid a few afternoons and get him working with a hammer and some nails. I worked with the coordinator of a high school program for gifted kids who was enthusiastic about finding mentors for these bright youngsters. Research into the problems of giftedness indicates that such kids often feel the loneliness of being different. The theory was that if they interacted with a gifted adult who was successful in the community, they would gain a more positive self-concept.

I applauded the idea, but suggested it would enhance the effort to select mentors based on similarities in conative makeup. I warned them that a Fact Finder student will drive a resistant Fact Finder nuts. The student will treat each session like an investigative reporter uncovering problems, and the mentor won't like being in a losing situation. One person who had been a mentor to many young people put it best: "If they don't have the basic instincts to start with, they won't get anything out of just following me around. They won't be able to adapt my methods to their future." The "right stuff" always equates to the right conative instincts. And when we can't find a mentor with a matching MO, there still is hope—finding common ground.

Common ground, conatively speaking, is a mode in which both people either insist or accommodate. To mutually resist a mode offers a common avoidance, rather than a way you'll be able to work together. As in bidding a bridge hand, it often works better to play in a suit in which both people have medium strength rather than one in which either partner is short-suited.

A stepmother was trying to find common ground with her husband's children. Claire, a fifteen-year-old, completed the Youth-KCI, while Brad, sixteen and working part-time, was ready for the regular version. Their MOs presented stepmother Katrina with a challenge.

| Katrina | 8255 |
| Claire | 3764 |
| Brad | 6842 |

Both youngsters needed far more structure than Katrina would provide of her own volition. She couldn't manufacture an ability to plan the activities they required, but she could discuss priorities with Brad, using both of their past experiences to gain insight into how they could manage daily routines when the kids were home, and regular communication when they were not. Claire was superb at translating those ideas into tailor-made systems. Her unique way of charting jobs allowed everyone to avoid the thing they liked to do least and kept all of them working as a team for just an hour a day, avoiding the weekend hassles that often had occurred.

Brad was pleased to have an excuse for not always doing the more physical tasks, Katrina passed on the Follow Thru function to a stepdaughter who felt a sense of accomplishment doing it, and all three accommodated the changes in routine through their Quick Start. Potential conflicts were sidestepped, at least most of the time, by trusting each others' instincts, respecting differences, and building on strengths—the same principles that prove effective in all relationships.

When otherwise conflicting people have Implementor in common, the advice I give centers on nonverbal activity. Build something together, work side by side in the yard, go fishing or camping. A Fact Finder woman was about to call off her engagement to a Quick Start who never wanted to discuss the problems they were having. After a day of sailing together they decided to give it another chance. They built a deck together, went on walks during which she didn't try to have discussions, and generally found they could settle differences best by meeting each other in the Implementor mode.

I was giving a speech to an auditorium of high school students when a young man in one of the front rows caught my eye. He was dressed in a wild, brilliantly colored get-up. His disheveled appearance was of a person going in a hundred directions at the same time. The group around him broke into laughter and applause when I asked if he was one of those people who wins a prize for originality but forgets to show up at the awards ceremony. He verified my hunch that everything I had said about Quick Starts fit him. Then he stood up, turned toward a back row, and said, "So, for God's sake, Leslie, leave me alone!" Leslie was his sister. Both kids were highly verbal, so their exchange was a better lesson than I could have planned.

"So now we have a name for you," Leslie said loudly, but calmly. "That doesn't make it all right to lose my tapes or leave the kitchen a mess, Danny."

"You care more about *things* than you do about me," he hollered back.

"That's not true," she responded. "I care about you enough to worry that you're growing up to be an irresponsible person. It's about time you got yourself under control."

Leslie thought her younger brother should start making lists of things he needed to do; he shouldn't go to bed at night without checking them; he should structure his time so that things got done; he shouldn't have so many activities that none ever get completed.

I asked Leslie if she'd mind coming down to the front. She carefully replaced her pencil in her purse, set her books down neatly, straightened the skirt of her coordinated outfit, ran her hand through her hair, and walked to the podium. Her irrepressible brother mimicked her so perfectly as he joined us in front of the group that there was tension in the auditorium. The two stared at each other for a moment, then burst into laughter.

The obvious love between them made it easier to sort out their differing approaches. A brother and sister are no more likely to have similar MOs than any other two people, and the effect of probable differences can be lifelong hassles, guilt, and frustration—or opportunity. The playground can become an invaluable training ground for learning to cope with conflicts. It can also broaden perspectives—and be a lot of fun.

I believed that Leslie and Danny were both able to at least accommodate in Fact Finder. I was therefore prepared to suggest they write down their disagreements, find examples of times when they worked things out between them, and discuss specific compromises. Although Danny might find it difficult to accommodate Leslie's need for Follow Thru, and she might be just as resistant to his Quick Start, if they could meet in the Fact Finder mode there was a good chance they could find practical ways to resolve their differences.

Sometimes, though, assumptions are dangerous. When they took the Youth-KCI, Leslie and Danny turned out to have a conflict in Fact Finder as well as Follow Thru and Quick Start (Leslie: 7823, Danny: 3296). "You see? I told you he was impossible," Leslie said, laughing and shaking her head.

The two came close to being conative opposites. Between them there was a resistance in each of the four modes. That left no common ground. I'd met with husbands and wives with similar problems. When it was a good marriage it was because they each gave each other lots of room to do things differently—and often apart from one another. They had a realistic attitude, a sense of humor, and the desire to make it work. In such situations they had to commit most or all of some modes to the other person. It takes that kind of effort for people in such a conatively polarized relationship to keep it working.

Vying for attention or respect or love, siblings will be working against a conative settlement. But when common purposes determine interactions, no amount of difference in MO is insurmountable, and realistic expectations can lead to positive results. Leslie and Danny had the desire. The KCI provided the reality. Humor reinforced the point.

## The Need to Be Known

Antonio, the hard-charging head of a mid-sized retailing company, while trying to keep the company in the black, was also trying to keep his family in one piece as it went through intense traumas. His twenty-two-year-old son, Tony, had a rare terminal blood disease. The boy wasn't expected to live more than another twelve to eighteen months, and was in and out of the hospital for periods of several weeks at a time. "Sure," Antonio said. "My business problems need your help, but nothing else matters when compared to Tony."

Antonio and Lucia were married when he was twenty-one and she only seventeen. They lived with her family until they got on their feet financially. Tony was born in the first year of their marriage and was always special to them. As Antonio went from stock boy to sales manager to owner of his own hardware store, he always dreamed of Tony's working with him. The boy showed early promise of being a great businessman when he came up with a brilliant idea for making T-shirts to sell at neighborhood birthday parties, weddings and such. As you might imagine, Antonio was immensely proud of him.

Gloria came along a year later and was always the good student and respectful daughter. She never made any waves until Tony's illness. Now she seemed to rebel at everything. Their youngest son, Raul, was a puzzle to Antonio. He'd always been quiet, and went along with his big brother whenever he could, but didn't strike out on his own. By the time he was sixteen, it wasn't clear who he was, except that he seemed to be withdrawing into his music more and more. He wasn't one of those rock music types who made a lot of noise and wore outlandish outfits, Antonio said. He kept more to himself and said he was composing, but for what Antonio didn't know.

Every member of the family filled out the KCI and these were the results:

| | |
|---------|------|
| Antonio | 4673 |
| Lucia   | 6644 |
| Tony    | 5285 |
| Gloria  | 8732 |
| Raul    | 4736 |

The diversity of the talents within the family was immediately obvious. So were some conflicts. What had been so revered as Tony's chip-off-the-old-block character was his match with Antonio's Quick Start. Both were innovators and would take risks. Tony was even more entrepreneurial than his Dad, whose MO made him perfectly suited to the service orientation of retailing and the system-intensity necessary for multiplying his efforts with several branch operations. Antonio had found his niche, but it's doubtful Tony would have been satisfied following in his father's footsteps. He had too much Quick Start to maintain an operation developed by anyone else. He would have a strong need to create his own unique success.

But, with Tony's illness, it was no longer a question of whether he was suited to the role that had always been assumed for him. Rather, now he was coping with the sad situation imposed on him, and he wasn't handling it well.

He was trying to be brave, and to tough it out to make things easier on his folks, but Tony was in distress beyond his physical pain. "I'm just lying here wasting away," he said. "My brain doesn't seem to know it's supposed to be sick. It wants to be *doing* something."

"Well, why don't you get busy and do something?" I asked.

"Okay, what?" he challenged me. "I know I'm not going to be around much longer. What's the point in tackling something that won't make any difference? It's hard to get my heart into it. I can't always remember things once I start them, and I get tired before I'm done with anything. Sometimes I can't even finish a letter I've started."

"You've never been one to finish things," I shot back, knowing Tony's 8 in Quick Start and 2 in Follow Thru. "Don't blame that on your illness. I'll bet every teacher you ever had complained that you didn't complete the assignment."

"You've got my number," he said. "But what does it matter now?"

No matter how ill a person is or how many days they have left on earth, they need goals, they have to free the productive force inside them and feed their soul. Tony was feeling useless. He had no purpose. His conative self wasn't impaired by his illness and his mental energy demanded release.

"You're a pretty strong-willed person," I goaded him.

"So why are you letting others dominate you? Why don't you come up with some solutions to your own problems? If you want to be productive, use some of your Quick Start and challenge the things that are bothering you. What is it you'd like to be doing with the mental energy you have available?"

After a moment's thought, he said, "Well, for one thing, I've been in this hospital enough to know a few things could be improved. I've also got some thoughts on some sales Dad could be making to places like this. Do you know the TVs don't have VCRs available? You can't rent movies or anything. I'd love it if Dad would get them to lease the equipment and set up a lending library of cassettes. It doesn't make any sense that they're not doing it. He could make good money at it, too."

That was just one of many projects he had in mind. But, every time I got him started contributing them, his mother would interject, "You need to rest. Don't tax your mind. You don't need to be worrying about those things."

She was trying hard to bring him peace in a way that she thought was best, but she was wrong. It took constant reinforcement for her to be able to handle Tony's need to be mentally active, and not try to suppress the natural force still inside him.

As a Facilitator, Lucia wanted to make everything better for everyone and didn't relate to Tony's insistent needs to do things for himself. Physically he was fatigued, but conatively, he was a young man full of mental energy that called out for expression.

Antonio grasped my message immediately and began challenging Tony. "Okay, quit lying there all day with things going around in your head that I need to know. Tell me how I can make more money. Maybe you can save me from having to work. Just tell me one of your genius gimmicks that'll make us all rich. What's the best way to get the people in this place to do what they ought to be doing, and how can we get them to pay for it?"

I started to hear a lot of laughter out of Tony and Antonio as they dickered over one idea or another. Tony told me his goal had been to come up with an invention that would make his family so wealthy they'd never have to work as hard as they had. "I'll leave something behind I can be proud of, you just wait and see." But I knew his efforts had made everyone proud already.

Over my shoulder I watched the reactions of Raul, who shared Tony's hands-on talents but didn't relate to his brother's general mode of operation. "But he won't have time to do anything with his ideas," he said. "It's just a trick to keep his mind off how sick he is. I bet it bothers him more than he says."

But Raul was an insistent Follow Thru, and, for him, closure mattered far more than it did to the Follow Thru resistant Tony. "My heart just breaks for him," Raul said. "And I can't stand it when he seems so excited about some dumb thing he'll never live to see happen anyway."

As he came to know the conative connection, it provided a great source of relief for Raul. First, it helped him understand that Tony's efforts weren't false, and that his brother had to be himself, even with a terminal illness. It also helped Raul see that he didn't have to emulate the older brother in their father's eyes. Antonio had never expected Raul to replace Tony or fill gaps in things the older son and father did together. But Raul hadn't known that. He had feared trying to fill an impossible role. "I can't live up to the legacy I know he's going to leave. I don't want to lose my brother, but I also don't want to be him."

Those innate, enduring conative qualities in Raul impelled him to persevere in being himself, even though his emotional desire was to hold his brother's place, to fill a void he knew was approaching for all of them. His retreat into himself made sense. He was protecting his very being.

In time, when his parents openly communicated their acceptance of who he was and their appreciation for his unique qualities, Raul let go of his fear. Eventually, he played one of his compositions for his parents and explained his intentions of pursuing a musical career.

"That's good," his father said, "We need someone around here who does something besides peddle wares. Maybe you'll class up our act."

I was pleased that my conative insights had been able to draw out the talents of Antonio's sons so their needs could be expressed and met, but that still left the now rebellious daughter Gloria. And Gloria wasn't talking or sharing in any of this. She had immersed herself in a relationship with a boyfriend she didn't bring home very often. She occassionally visited Tony when he was hospitalized, but only briefly. There was an awkwardness between them, and a withdrawal from the family. I knew she was a person who would not normally act so inappropriately (not with an 8 in Fact Finder) and I was aware that this highly stressful and disruptive situation would cause confusion in her mind. Her Follow Thru insistence demanded stability in her life. Perhaps she was looking for that stability from outside the family because of the disruptions taking place within it.

Gloria needed help, but I couldn't do it alone. Because of the emotional overlay of the problems, we needed to involve a therapist. Unfortunately, most therapists don't know or understand the conative connection, unless by pure intuition. It's not been part of their training or experience. Gloria found some help understanding her emotions through a therapy process, but she still had to act on them.

I helped Gloria deal with her internal conative drives by encouraging her Fact Finder insistence. I had her bombarding me with questions until finally she said, "I'm not completely convinced about this conative stuff, but I can't deny the effect on others in my family. It also helps me see how I've been the odd man out in the group and why they do things so differently."

Shortly thereafter, she made the all-important first step of writing a lengthy letter to Tony, in which she detailed the many things they had done together which had meant so much to her. She acted on her Fact Finder need to bring the past together with the present. It gave her the perspective she needed to begin a journey back into the family circle.

After Tony's death I received a very special letter, one he had written and addressed to me before his final coma. It simply said, "Thanks for giving me back the dignity I thought was lost to me. I feel better knowing I was known."

# EPILOGUE

Now that you know about the conative connection, you have the same responsibility I did after the car accident I mentioned in the Preface. I couldn't remain ignorant or cognitively unqualified, because I had to communicate, to reintegrate the three parts of my mind so I could fulfill my sense of purpose.

Just reading about this new concept isn't enough. You'll need to try it. You'll need to reach down and pull up the blanket. Discovering your own MO through the KCI is one action you can take. Another is to confront problems and opportunities in conative terms. Then, when you're ready to commit some mental energy to the effort, you'll be able to use the conative connection to make a difference.

I knew about the conative connection before the drunk driver smashed into my life. The KCI had already proven predictive of people's actions, but, until I had to function with impaired cognitive ability and gyrating emotions, I didn't fully appreciate the extent to which the creative instincts determine how we will and won't handle whatever may come our way.

Despite all the pain, expense, and uncertainty, the time I was forced to spend recuperating was actually a gift. I had always recommended brief periods of quiet for everyone, turning off the cognitive button now and then. With the exception of working in my garden, I had never found it all that easy to practice what I preached. While I struggled to put the accident and its aftermath behind me I reentered the working world with a certain degree of regret.

Odd as it may sound, I actually enjoyed my hospital stay. It was fun to use gadgets I had never seen before, enjoyable to be able to share feelings with initially ill-at-ease visitors and immerse myself in newfound friendships by acting with the naivete of those we label retarded.

When the intellect is not asking why, trying to discover hidden meanings or questioning motives, accepting people or events at face value is easy, and a great pleasure. At the time, I lacked the intellectual capacity to truly analyze my situation. I did not stand in judgement. I did not question, reason, discern, or even understand. I simply accepted.

Having been blessed with a period in which I did not think clearly, I have a clear understanding of what it is, not just to think, but to act and to feel. What I know for certain now is that the integration of the three faculties of the mind is the key to being whole. I had thought, perhaps as you still do, that one can learn to control actions, that they are modified by experience and education. Reading this book won't change your mind. It's only when you test the theories that I've presented that you'll discover the inborn nature of your own power—that your capabilities have been and will always be ready and waiting for your use.

I have dealt here with the implications of the conative connection for personal and organizational development.

The next step is to apply the Kolbe Concept to major areas of concern. The potential of integrating the conative into education alone staggers the imagination. When we begin building on individual strengths instead of expecting conformity, the intuitive sense that not all children learn the same way will become an instructional reality. It will take a massive effort to train teachers and revise materials, but it will be the essential reform we have until now only given lip service.

The day will come when Quick Starts aren't penalized for trying it another way and Implementors' needs aren't ignored except in sports and shop. Teaching will have a wider appeal when we open education to a broader spectrum of talents. Classroom burnout will be less rampant.

For medicine, the conative dimension offers an untapped reservoir of techniques for speeding the healing process. With its generalizable insights, conation allows health care professionals to establish a much deeper level of empathy with their patients, without discarding the emotional detachment needed to meet the demands of constantly dealing with death and disease.

The relationship between physical and mental energies still requires research, as do many questions regarding the applications for the conative connection. Having studied conation and intelligence, I am satisfied that not only is there no correlation between them, but that retarded peoples' need for conative self-determination is just as great as others'. The help that can be provided handicapped people by building on their instincts requires immediate attention.

It will take collaboration—acting in synergy—to carry out the multitude of studies that may prove there are conative solutions for issues such as drug and alcohol abuse, crime, suicide, poverty, aging, and power struggles that have led to economic and political wars.

This book is but the tip of the iceberg. By studying the implications of the conative connection and our ability to maximize the use of our brainpower, we will each fulfill our responsibility to enhance our individual efforts and increase our contributions to society.

# APPENDIX: HOW TO GET YOUR KCI RESULTS

One of my earliest efforts with conation was a self-scored index which, unfortunately, did not work. Arriving at an accurate picture of a person's MO is not as simple as adding up all the Fact Finder "mosts" and subtracting the Fact Finder "leasts." It is a complex process involving weighted factors to convert raw scores to predictive results, and other statistical paraphernalia to translate data into the percentage of mental energy a person has in each mode. Over several years of experimentation I found the most practical and reliable measure was the practical KCI approach.

KCI results help people target their mental energy into productive career paths, avoid stressful situations, and reduce conflict in their interactions. Individuals who receive an interpretation of their results, either in a seminar or in a written form from my office, confirm the descriptions of their most probable actions 98 percent of the time. They affirm that the results quantify how they will and won't tackle tasks. Oddly enough, when friends, family members, or co-workers try to guess the outcome, they are off by 10 percent in one or more modes more than 75 percent of the time, and individuals are unable to predict their own results more than 50 percent of the time. One reason people have trouble quantifying their natural talents is that they are unused to thinking in terms of conation.

I'm often asked if a KCI result would change if you were in a different circumstance—a new job, more educated, a changed environment. The answer is no. The KCI is not like a personality test which gives differing results depending upon mood and circumstances. You only need to take the KCI once—unless you are among the approximately 15 percent of the population in conative crisis. We've given second, third, even fourth KCIs to people after they've undergone significantly changed circumstances. The results were within 5 percent for each mode—except for those who had come out of or gone into conative crisis. Less than 1 percent of a sample of 20,000 people changed from insistent in a mode to resistant in it. In every one of those few cases, the people were trying to fill it out as if they were another person—usually a boss whose shoes they hoped to fill.

Executives in one Fortune 100 company were sure they could change MOs. "After six months in our intensive training program," I was told, "people yield to our 'culture.' They become what we want them to be." I took them on. We tested participants before and after a program in which the company presumed it had taught them "to be more innovative." The change was less than 2 percent, well within the KCI's margin of error.

While you're welcome to try to figure out what it might mean to answer a certain way on some of the questions on the KCI, let me caution you against drawing conclusions based on that kind of armchair analysis. The KCI is not a parlor game. A properly evaluated score can be a valuable tool in making career choices and other important life decisions, but only an accredited Kolbe Concepts professional can give you that evaluation.

The KCI that follows was designed for those aged sixteen years or older who have had some work experience. Information regarding the Youth-KCI, Job-KCI, and foreign-language versions is available from the Kolbe Concepts office listed below.

If you would like to know your KCI score, answer the questions on the following pages. Then send a photocopy of those pages, along with a check

Make cheque payable to:

C.E. Corporate Services Inc.
#802 – 1200 Burrard St.
Vancouver, B.C.
V6Z 2C7

* Please note that only one KCI is available at this special book offering price of $49.95 US or $60.00 Canadian.

## Kolbe Conative Index

Since there are no good or bad MOs, there are no right or wrong answers here. For each item, you are to pick the action behavior you would *most* likely take and the one you would be *least* likely to take. Indicate each by placing an X in the appropriate columns in front of the options you select.

*Example*

MOST    LEAST

**A. If I were describing my hobbies, I would include:**

| MOST | LEAST | |
|------|-------|---|
| X | ____ | sports |
| ____ | ____ | collecting or doing word puzzles |
| ____ | X | fast-paced projects |
| ____ | ____ | fashion or self-improvement |

The important thing to keep in mind is how you would naturally act, rather than how others want you to behave or how circumstances might force you to act. When in doubt, add the phrase "If free to be myself . . ."

While some questions may not seem to relate to you, and while you may have several alternatives to choose, for accurate results it is important to mark one *"most"* and one *"least"* for *every* question. Remember: the results of the Kolbe Conative Index are always positive, because they identify your natural talents.

# Kolbe Conative Index

DATE _____

NAME (Please print) _____

HOME ADDRESS: STREET _____

CITY, STATE, ZIP _____

HOME PHONE NUMBER _____

BUSINESS ADDRESS: STREET _____

CITY, STATE, ZIP _____

BUSINESS PHONE NUMBER _____

SEX: M / F

AGE: _____ Under 20 _____ 21–30 _____ 31–40

_____ 41–50 _____ 51–65 _____ Over 65

EDUCATION: _____ high school graduate

_____ some college

_____ 4-yr college graduate

_____ postgraduate

ANNUAL INCOME:

_____ $0–14,999 _____ $15,000–19,999 _____ $20,000–29,999

_____ $30,000–39,999 _____ $40,000–59,999 _____ $60,000 +

JOB TITLE _____

COMPANY _____

TYPE OF BUSINESS/INDUSTRY _____

NUMBER YEARS EMPLOYED IN THAT COMPANY _____

NUMBER YEARS IN THAT TYPE OF POSITION _____

| MOST | LEAST | (Mark one most and one least for each item.) |

**1. If I were helping others to learn to use a tool, I would:**

___ ___ encourage trial-and-error effort
___ ___ be sure they had the directions
___ ___ explain why it works the way it does
___ ___ have them watch me use it

**2. If I were deciding whether an idea was any good, I would consider its:**

___ ___ practicality
___ ___ efficiency
___ ___ impact
___ ___ durability

**3. If I were describing a business office, I would mention:**

___ ___ degree of organization, type of layout, neatness
___ ___ as many specific details as I could remember
___ ___ quality of equipment and materials
___ ___ the general atmosphere

**4. If I were setting up a display, I would:**

___ ___ be concerned that everything look orderly and function smoothly
___ ___ try clever, unique ways to do it
___ ___ do all the necessary planning in advance
___ ___ want to set it up personally

**5. If I were told to hurry finishing a project, I would:**

___ ___ enjoy the challenge
___ ___ decide what could be done properly
___ ___ work diligently until time was up
___ ___ consider craftsmanship most important

**MOST    LEAST**

6. If I were exploring a new object, I would:
\_\_\_\_  \_\_\_\_  check how it was made
\_\_\_\_  \_\_\_\_  approach it systematically
\_\_\_\_  \_\_\_\_  examine it in detail
\_\_\_\_  \_\_\_\_  have a strong first impression

7. If I were selecting clothes to wear, I would pick those that are:
\_\_\_\_  \_\_\_\_  comfortable
\_\_\_\_  \_\_\_\_  necessary and appropriate
\_\_\_\_  \_\_\_\_  well coordinated
\_\_\_\_  \_\_\_\_  fun to wear

8. If I won a prize for artistic effort, it would be for:
\_\_\_\_  \_\_\_\_  neatness and interesting patterns
\_\_\_\_  \_\_\_\_  realism, perspective or good detail
\_\_\_\_  \_\_\_\_  good use of color
\_\_\_\_  \_\_\_\_  model building, sculpture

9. If I were concentrating on a single effort, I would be:
\_\_\_\_  \_\_\_\_  systematic
\_\_\_\_  \_\_\_\_  intuitive
\_\_\_\_  \_\_\_\_  skillful
\_\_\_\_  \_\_\_\_  thorough

10. If I were working on a puzzle, I would prefer one that requires:
\_\_\_\_  \_\_\_\_  quick thinking
\_\_\_\_  \_\_\_\_  putting physical pieces together
\_\_\_\_  \_\_\_\_  good memory for facts
\_\_\_\_  \_\_\_\_  patience

MOST    LEAST

**11.  If I were picking a category to win a contest, I would win for:**

_____  _____  craftsmanship
_____  _____  neatness
_____  _____  originality
_____  _____  being the most realistic

**12.  If I were explaining an idea, I would be:**

_____  _____  spontaneous
_____  _____  methodical
_____  _____  technical
_____  _____  tactful

**13.  If I ran a business, I would:**

_____  _____  provide steady performance
_____  _____  make carefully thought-out decisions
_____  _____  develop new products, be innovative
_____  _____  maintain high quality workmanship

**14.  If I were trying to get off the hook for something, my arguments would be:**

_____  _____  consistent
_____  _____  humorous
_____  _____  thorough
_____  _____  brief

**15.  If I were teased about a characteristic, it would be:**

_____  _____  touchiness
_____  _____  impulsiveness
_____  _____  preciseness
_____  _____  predictability

MOST    LEAST

**16. If I were working as a member of a group, I would:**

——  ——  tackle physical tasks
——  ——  have lots of ideas
——  ——  be efficient
——  ——  outline goals and objectives

**17. If I were criticized, it would be for being too:**

——  ——  impatient
——  ——  sensitive
——  ——  structured
——  ——  argumentative

**18. If I earned recognition, it probably would be for:**

——  ——  speed and cleverness
——  ——  strength and endurance
——  ——  dependability and design
——  ——  judgment and accuracy

**19. If I could, I would have:**

——  ——  security
——  ——  upgraded equipment
——  ——  commissions
——  ——  expense account

**20. If I were choosing my own work situation, I would want to:**

——  ——  do the work myself
——  ——  have others available for brainstorming
——  ——  be able to delegate
——  ——  have the work flow to me smoothly

**MOST    LEAST**

**21. If I were demonstrating my talents, it would be with:**

____  ____  words

____  ____  data

____  ____  taking risks

____  ____  using strength

**22. If I were solving a difficult problem, I would rely most heavily on my:**

____  ____  skill

____  ____  research

____  ____  structuring it

____  ____  experimentation

**23. If I were setting standards, I would find it important that they be:**

____  ____  demonstrable

____  ____  uniform

____  ____  flexible

____  ____  measurable

**24. If a task required my best work, I would want to:**

____  ____  double-check results

____  ____  practice it

____  ____  take it on as a challenge

____  ____  do adequate research

**25. If I were asked to prove my point, I would:**

____  ____  show it in some form

____  ____  explain my method

____  ____  explain the pros and cons

____  ____  explain the benefits

MOST   LEAST

**26. If I were caught between a rock and a hard place, I would:**
———  ———  evaluate the situation
———  ———  try to push them apart
———  ———  tackle one anyway
———  ———  arrange it as well as possible

**27. If something in the system didn't work, I would:**
———  ———  work around it
———  ———  repair it
———  ———  find out why
———  ———  report it

**28. If I believed something important could be made to help mankind, I would want to:**
———  ———  investigate it
———  ———  design it
———  ———  sell or promote it
———  ———  build it

**29. If I were measuring a project's potential, I would want to:**
———  ———  have fixed methods of measurement
———  ———  get as much background information as possible
———  ———  trust my instincts
———  ———  stick to personal standards

**30. If I were in charge of a project, I would want to be sure I could:**
———  ———  meet specifications
———  ———  use quality materials
———  ———  be cost-effective
———  ———  add my own ideas

**MOST    LEAST**

**31. If I were assigned one task, I would prefer:**

\_\_\_\_  \_\_\_\_  researching

\_\_\_\_  \_\_\_\_  constructing

\_\_\_\_  \_\_\_\_  promoting

\_\_\_\_  \_\_\_\_  planning

**32. If I could learn in any manner, I would choose to learn from:**

\_\_\_\_  \_\_\_\_  taking my chances

\_\_\_\_  \_\_\_\_  practice

\_\_\_\_  \_\_\_\_  books

\_\_\_\_  \_\_\_\_  examples

**33. If I got into trouble, it would be because I:**

\_\_\_\_  \_\_\_\_  was bored

\_\_\_\_  \_\_\_\_  couldn't keep my hands off things

\_\_\_\_  \_\_\_\_  resisted change

\_\_\_\_  \_\_\_\_  wanted to know too much

**34. If I could do things my way, they would get done:**

\_\_\_\_  \_\_\_\_  realistically

\_\_\_\_  \_\_\_\_  physically

\_\_\_\_  \_\_\_\_  rapidly

\_\_\_\_  \_\_\_\_  cautiously

**35. If I can, I avoid:**

\_\_\_\_  \_\_\_\_  guessing

\_\_\_\_  \_\_\_\_  discussions

\_\_\_\_  \_\_\_\_  restrictions

\_\_\_\_  \_\_\_\_  interruptions

MOST    LEAST

36. **If free to be myself, I would get things done by:**
—— —— researching
—— —— planning ahead
—— —— hard work
—— —— taking on challenges

For each of the following statements, indicate whether you strongly agree, agree, are undecided, disagree, or strongly disagree with the information stated by circling the number from 10–1 (most agree to most disagree).

1. **I plan to use the conative connection to assist me in:**

A.  Personal Awareness

| AGREE | | | | UNDECIDED | | | | DISAGREE | |
|---|---|---|---|---|---|---|---|---|---|
| 10 | 9 | 8 | 7 | 6 | 5 | 4 | 3 | 2 | 1 |

B.  Organizational Development

| AGREE | | | | UNDECIDED | | | | DISAGREE | |
|---|---|---|---|---|---|---|---|---|---|
| 10 | 9 | 8 | 7 | 6 | 5 | 4 | 3 | 2 | 1 |

C.  Management Training

| AGREE | | | | UNDECIDED | | | | DISAGREE | |
|---|---|---|---|---|---|---|---|---|---|
| 10 | 9 | 8 | 7 | 6 | 5 | 4 | 3 | 2 | 1 |

D.  Career Decisions

| AGREE | | | | UNDECIDED | | | | DISAGREE | |
|---|---|---|---|---|---|---|---|---|---|
| 10 | 9 | 8 | 7 | 6 | 5 | 4 | 3 | 2 | 1 |

E.  Adult Relationships

| AGREE | | | | UNDECIDED | | | | DISAGREE | |
|---|---|---|---|---|---|---|---|---|---|
| 10 | 9 | 8 | 7 | 6 | 5 | 4 | 3 | 2 | 1 |

F.  Retirement Decisions

| AGREE | | | | UNDECIDED | | | | DISAGREE | |
|---|---|---|---|---|---|---|---|---|---|
| 10 | 9 | 8 | 7 | 6 | 5 | 4 | 3 | 2 | 1 |

G. Succession Decisions

| AGREE | | | | UNDECIDED | | | | DISAGREE | |
|---|---|---|---|---|---|---|---|---|---|
| 10 | 9 | 8 | 7 | 6 | 5 | 4 | 3 | 2 | 1 |

2. I am pleased with my career path.

| AGREE | | | | UNDECIDED | | | | DISAGREE | |
|---|---|---|---|---|---|---|---|---|---|
| 10 | 9 | 8 | 7 | 6 | 5 | 4 | 3 | 2 | 1 |

3. My current performance gives me a strong sense of achievement.

| AGREE | | | | UNDECIDED | | | | DISAGREE | |
|---|---|---|---|---|---|---|---|---|---|
| 10 | 9 | 8 | 7 | 6 | 5 | 4 | 3 | 2 | 1 |

4. I am under a lot of stress at work (or school).

| AGREE | | | | UNDECIDED | | | | DISAGREE | |
|---|---|---|---|---|---|---|---|---|---|
| 10 | 9 | 8 | 7 | 6 | 5 | 4 | 3 | 2 | 1 |

5. Often I'm required to work against my natural grain.

| AGREE | | | | UNDECIDED | | | | DISAGREE | |
|---|---|---|---|---|---|---|---|---|---|
| 10 | 9 | 8 | 7 | 6 | 5 | 4 | 3 | 2 | 1 |

6. Circumstances are preventing me from being myself right now.

| AGREE | | | | UNDECIDED | | | | DISAGREE | |
|---|---|---|---|---|---|---|---|---|---|
| 10 | 9 | 8 | 7 | 6 | 5 | 4 | 3 | 2 | 1 |

# GLOSSARY

**Accommodating**   Having between 4 and 6 units of mental energy in a given Action Mode, indicating an ability to use the mode as needed.

**Action Modes**   Four distinct clusters of behavior which result from acting on instinct.

- **Fact Finder**   The Action Mode that deals with detail and complexity and provides the perspective of experience.
- **Follow Thru**   The Action Mode that deals with structure and order and provides focus and continuity.
- **Quick Start**   The Action Mode that deals with originality and risk-taking and provides intuition and a sense of vision.
- **Implementor**   The Action Mode that deals with physical space and ability to operate manually, and provides durability and a sense of the tangible.

**Affective**   One of the three parts of the mind; pertaining to or arising from feeling or emotion.

**Cognitive**   One of the three parts of the mind; deals with knowledge, skills, and intellectual processes.

**Conation**   One of the three parts of the mind; controls conscious effort and strives to carry out volitional acts.

**Conative clones**  People with similar modes of operation or ways of doing things.

**Conative conflict**  Stress resulting from natural differences in how people function.

**Conative crisis**  The loss of ability to express or recognize one's own conative nature; loss of sense of self.

**Conative crunch**  Temporary thwarting of goal-directed actions.

**Creative instincts**  Inborn tendencies to initiate action through probing, patterning, innovating, and demonstrating.

**Depletion**  Loss of productivity caused by people trying to work against their natural grain to accomplish organizational goals.

**Facilitator**  A person with all four Action Modes in the mid-range.

**Inertia**  Loss of productivity caused by uniformity of action among people in an organization.

**Insistence**  Strong-willed behavior resulting from high levels of energy in one Action Mode.

**Job-KCI**  A pencil-and-paper instrument that measures job performance expectations.

**Kolbe Conative Index (KCI)**  A pencil-and-paper instrument that quantifies the degree of natural talent an individual possesses in each Action Mode.

**Knacks**  How people instinctively deal with detail, structure, risk, and tangible effort.

**The Kolbe Concept**  Concept that helps discover natural talents and build on those strengths.

**Leisure**  Activity that does not involve striving.

**Meltdown**  A loss of productivity caused by unrealistic

pressure for workers to perform according to organizational requirements.

**Mental energy** Capacity of conative striving mechanisms available for goal-directed activity.

**Modus Operandi (MO)** An individual's instinctive way of taking action.

**Polarization** Loss of productivity that occurs when groups within an organization have significantly different approaches to problem solving.

**Recreation** Free-time activity that involves striving.

**Resistance** The unwillingness to act through an Action Mode.

**Strain** Stress resulting from a person's unrealistic self-expectations of how he or she will perform.

**Tension** Stress resulting from another person's unrealistic expectations for how a person will perform.

# INDEX